JEFF VANDERSTELT

ONE EIGHTY

A RETURN TO DISCIPLE-MAKING

ΞXPONΞNTIAL

Exponential is a growing movement of activists committed to the multiplication of healthy new churches. Exponential Resources spotlights actionable principles, ideas, and solutions for the accelerated multiplication of healthy, reproducing faith communities. For more information, visit exponential.org.

One Eighty: A Return to Disciple-Making

ISBN: 978-1-62424-121-5 (paperback)
ISBN: 978-1-62424-118-5 (ebook/epub)
Editor: Karen Cain
Cover and interior design: Sabir Robinson

DEDICATION

This book is the result of years of learning with broken people in imperfect spaces that allowed a broken and imperfect man to try and fail, live and learn, hurt and be hurt, seek forgiveness and heal, and keep moving toward what Jesus wants for his disciples and his Church.

The people and spaces include the people of Olivet Evangelical Free Church in Muskegon, First Christian Reformed Church in Seattle, Christ Community Church in St. Charles, Willow Creek Community Church in South Barrington, Doxa Church in West Seattle, Soma Church in Tacoma, Doxa Church in Bellevue, and the microchurch of which we are presently a part.

I've learned over the years that most relationships are short-term. That's sad, but it's true. But a few relationships are for a lifetime. Sadly, I've often invested my best time and energy in the short-term relationships, while the long-term have suffered the cost. In these later years, I realize that those who get the best of me are the ones who aren't leaving me.

Thank you, Jayne, Haylee, Maggie, and Caleb for loving me even though you certainly paid the greatest price for my failures and my learning.

Thankfully, we are all still together, healing alongside each other.

I love you deeply, and I thank God for you daily.

EXPONENTIAL⌐

EX⌐
24

2024 GLOBAL CONFERENCE

ONEIGHTY⌐

THE RETURN TO DISCIPLE-MAKING

march 4–7 · orlando

REGISTER NOW AT
exponential.org/2024

SATURATE'S
DISCIPLE-MAKING LAB

A ONE-YEAR JOURNEY FOR YOU AND YOUR LEADERSHIP TEAM TO COLLABORATIVELY:

- Develop a definition of a disciple of Jesus.
- Build a unique disciple-making pathway for your context.
- Cultivate the environments and culture that support disciple-making.
- Design transferable tools that lead to disciples who make disciples in your church.

INCLUDED IN THIS EXPERIENCE:

- Two in-person intensives for you and your team with Jeff Vanderstelt and Ben Connelly.
- Monthly live online workshops.
- Unlimited access to Saturate's full library of resources including videos, ebooks, courses, discussion guides, and more to equip you on your disciple-making journey.

JEFF VANDERSTELT

As the founder of the Soma Family of Churches and Visionary Director of Saturate, Jeff Vanderstelt will bring 34 years of ministry experience and thought-leadership to your journey.

BEN CONNELLY

Ben Connelly is a master at creating and facilitating learning environments and has done so through such roles as church planter, pastor, author, professor, Director of Plant Fort Worth, and Founder of The Equipping Group.

saturatetheworld.com/all-training

Contents

Foreword

"We have not done a good job of discipling our people."

If there is one post-pandemic confession I have heard church leaders in the United States make more than any other it is this: "We have not done a good job of discipling our people." Repeatedly I hear leaders of big churches and small churches and everything in between say, "We have got to get back to focusing on disciple-making." As a local church pastor, I join the confessional chorus and admit that we need to return to disciple-making! For that reason, *One-eighty: A Return to Disciple-Making* is one of the most important church leadership books of our time and the theme of all our 2024 Exponential conferences.

One of the great privileges of leading Exponential is that I have the honor of selecting and asking someone to write our annual theme book. It is kind of like being a general manager of a sports team and knowing you have the first pick in the upcoming draft. When it came to this topic, one name immediately came to mind as my top selection—Jeff Vanderstelt.

Why Jeff? Let me give you two reasons Jeff was my first choice. First, Jeff is a pastor and a maker of disciple-makers. Jeff has pastored at some of the largest and most influential churches in the country. Jeff has also pastored in some of the most innovative churches consisting of a network of multiplying missional communities. Jeff has also pastored in turnaround churches whose better days seemed to be behind rather than ahead. In a variety of contexts, as a pastor, Jeff has led those churches to become disciple-making churches. A big reason they became disciple-making communities is because Jeff is a disciple-maker. He lives a life of a disciple-maker. He is buying what he is selling! He makes disciples.

Second, Jeff is both a thought leader and a practitioner. Jeff has written widely and thought deeply on this topic of discipleship and disciple-making. I remember my own trip from Chicago to the northwest corner of the United States to see first-hand how Jeff was creating a disciple-making culture. What I saw was brilliant, biblical, and authentic. I borrowed as much as I could. He not only did that for me, but he has done that for thousands of churches and tens of thousands of church leaders. With each of these churches and with each of these leaders, he offers real-life practical ideas and tools that can be a great help in making disciples of Jesus.

So, when Jeff said "yes" to writing this book, I already knew it would be a great resource. We started by looking at the framework from our outstanding 2013 Exponential resource,

DiscipleShift: Five Steps That Help Your Church to Make Disciples Who Make Disciples by Jim Putman and Bobby Harrington. I still highly recommend it! From there, Jeff wrote *One-eighty* that highlights clearly and profoundly five important shifts that our churches must make if we are to accomplish the mission of Jesus.

The book brings together deep thought-provoking principles on disciple-making that are crucial for any disciple-making leader. These principles are paired with practical insights and helpful prompts in five workbook style sections to serve as a catalyst for implementation. The content of this book does not disappoint. Read and apply the contents of this book, and your church will return to its first calling—disciple-making.

This book gives me hope that in the not-too-distant future church leaders, current confession of "We have not done a good job of discipling our people" will be replaced with a rallying cry of "We are making disciples who make disciples!" I long for and look forward to that day.

Thank you, Jeff, for dedicating your life's work to this ultimately worthwhile cause. Thank you for doing it in a way that is helpful to other leaders like me. And thank you for writing this book. It is an honor for Exponential to share *One-eighty: A Return to Disciple-Making* with the world.

Dave Ferguson
President and Co-founder
Exponential

It's Time for a Shift

Prior to 2020, during a time of training, I would often ask, "If for some reason the church you lead was no longer permitted to gather together in a building, how prepared are your people to go and be the church on mission, making disciples without attending a weekly gathering?" I had always had some kind of religious persecution in mind when I asked the question. Never did I think of a pandemic. Then COVID-19 happened, and most of the world was not allowed to gather in large groups for an extended period of time. It was a wake-up call to the Church, as we discovered how prepared or unprepared we were.

Some churches thrived during COVID. People engaged in serving their neighbors, they met together regularly in smaller groups (in whatever size was allowed), and they shared with others the reason they served and loved people like Jesus had served and loved them. COVID-19, like the persecution of the church in Jerusalem, propelled many people on mission like never before. It was a catalyst that released trained followers of Jesus to step more fully into their calling. I heard many stories from church leaders about how the people they trained stepped out and up in their obedience to Jesus' call to make disciples.

And yet, I also listened and watched many other leaders panic and rage, as they had very little hope that the people they led would continue to follow and obey Jesus faithfully without a regular weekly gathering. And sadly, many of them did not. We witnessed many people leave the church and their faith. We also observed Christians become more divided than ever as they fought and rejected one another. Sadly, the world watched far too many Christians become more known for criticism and hatred than grace and love.

Most were not prepared. The Church was not very mature, according to how Jesus measured disciples—by their love for others, including their enemies. We were found wanting when it comes to making disciples of Jesus who would be known for their love.

We could spend an entire book simply unpacking what we discovered during the years 2020–2022, and I imagine many will be written. But that is not the goal of this book. The assumption of this book is that many Christians did come to realize that we have dropped the ball on making disciples of Jesus who can in turn make disciples who resemble the life and character of Jesus. COVID-19 was a check-up visit to the divine physician's office for church health. I believe the Spirit of God revealed to us that many churches and ministries had not made disciple-making disciples.

It seems we may have done a better job creating consumers who showed their true cards when the goods and services they were used to consuming had been taken away. We had become proficient at creating gatherings, leading musical worship, preaching compelling sermons, and designing attractive programs. And people were gladly attending and taking what they wanted. But when what they wanted was taken away, they went away. What could have been one of the greatest opportunities for the Church to display the good news of Jesus to their neighbors was lost on people who had not been trained and prepared for the moment. Ironically, although making disciples is the clear mission of the Church, when asked, most churches say that making disciples who make disciples is still their biggest weakness.

How can this be, if making disciples is the core mission of the Church? We will unpack five reasons in this book, each of which describes a shift we need to make:

- We need to shift from just reaching people to making disciples.
- We need to shift from merely informing disciples to equipping disciple-makers.
- We need to shift from calling people to attend programs and events to leading people to truly attach to God and others.
- We need to shift from unhealthy striving to thriving as Spirit-empowered disciples and emotionally healthy leaders.
- And finally, we need to shift from merely accumulating people into our buildings and programs to deploying disciple-making disciples to the ends of the earth.

We need to do a 180 and get back to the basics of Jesus' command to make disciples who make disciples.

Some of you are already familiar with the 5 shift framework. In 2013, Jim Putman and Bobby Harrington worked with Exponential to address this same problem at the 2013 Exponential Conference. They created a framework which they also put into a book called *DiscipleShift: Five Steps to Help Your Church Make Disciples Who Make Disciples*. The framework identified five shifts we need to make in order to get back to disciple-making. Since then, they have also developed DiscipleShift seminars that have helped many leaders and churches make the shift back to disciple-making. In the spring of 2023, Dave Ferguson reached out and asked if I would be willing to take the original five shift framework and rework it for our post-Covid context for the 2023 Exponential Conference. That work led to this book. In this book, you will notice some similarities and some differences from the original five shift framework they originally developed.

I share Bobby and Jim's passion for helping the church make the shift. For that reason, I wrote this book for anyone who wants to get back to what Jesus saved and called us to be and do. Some of you presently lead a church or a particular part of the church. It's time for you to lead the shift. Some of you have become disillusioned with the Church because she seems so far away from what Jesus called her to be. Don't give up. Jesus promised he would build his church, and the gates of hell (and our past mistakes) will not prevail against his work.

You can be a part of the way Jesus accomplishes his work. Some of you have wondered whether you have a role to play.

You do. The Church is the people of God saved by the power of God and filled with the presence of God for the purposes of God in this world. If you have come to Jesus and received the Spirit, you are part of Jesus' body, the Church.

It's time for all of us who love and follow Jesus to get back to what he saved and called us to be: disciples of Jesus who make disciples of Jesus. Let's make the shift and chart a new future for the Church together.

SHIFT #1

FROM REACHING TO MAKING

FROM REACHING TO MAKING

The first shift we need to make is from simply reaching more people to grow the size of our ministry or church to actually making disciples. Otherwise we risk slipping into a purely pragmatic, attractional approach.

Attracting people is not in itself wrong if we are attracting them to Jesus and calling them to follow and submit their lives to him. Sadly, too many ministries and churches have primarily measured their success by how many people attend their events. This often leads to a "do-whatever-it-takes-to-attract-more-and-more-people" mentality. In many cases, the ministry or church becomes more of an entertainment industry than a disciple-making ministry. In the worst of cases, churches avoid speaking truth and end up presenting a "genie in a bottle" Jesus who grants your every wish but never calls you to surrender your life to his will and purposes. These ministries and churches do attract, and they often grow larger; but they don't make mature disciples of Jesus who are able to make disciples of Jesus.

Another problem we must face is that many people believe you can become a Christian and never become a disciple of Jesus, as if there are two tiers within Christianity. Sadly, too many have been led to believe that the goal is merely conversion to Christianity. But the goal according to Scripture is being reconciled into a life-changing relationship with God through the work of Jesus Christ by the power of the Spirit, which leads to us being conformed to the image of Christ. This is the abundant life Jesus promised for all who would come to him, abide in him, and live life with him.

The Church needs to return to what Jesus commanded: Go make disciples of all nations. This invitation is not for the select few. It is for the whole church and requires the whole church being mobilized on mission everyday, making disciples of Jesus together.

One Eighty: A Return to Disciple-Making

CHAPTER ONE

What Is a Disciple?

What is a disciple? How do we know whether we are being faithful in making disciples? We need to be sure we have a clear definition of what a disciple is if we are going to determine whether or not we are effectively making them.

Defining the Target

My brother Marty works for Proctor and Gamble, and over the years he has overseen several products from feminine care to laundry detergents to baby care products (what he presently oversees for North America). During each campaign, he knew what each product was supposed to do, how it worked, how it was made from start to finish, and how to uniquely communicate and market that product to different cultural contexts. Presently, one of his key products is Pampers diapers. Everyone under his authority knows what they are and how they are made.

Good diapers are important, as every parent with little ones knows. And making a quality product is important. However, the eternal value of a diaper and a human soul have no comparison. Each time I listen to my brother describe all that goes into a product he has ever overseen, I ponder to myself, *Does the Church think this thoroughly about making disciples?*

Every Christian is called to the work of making disciples. But do we know what a disciple *is? Do we know how a disciple is made?*

Think about the ministry or church you lead or participate in. Do you have a clear, shared definition of a disciple? Do you have a definite process for how disciples are made in your context, and does everyone know how to personally engage in it?

Why is a definition important? Because we cannot make what we cannot state.

The Definition According to Jesus

When Jesus launched his public ministry, he called his first disciples beside the Sea of Galilee. He saw Simon (also known as Peter) and his brother Andrew casting a net into the sea because they were fishermen. Jesus said to them, "Come, follow me … and I will send you out to fish for people" (Matthew 4:19).

I've discovered in talking to my brother that every product P&G makes is uniquely designed for the cultural context in which it is sold. Tide detergent made and sold in the USA is different from Tide made and sold in Japan. The product does the same thing overall, but it works differently because the chemical makeup of the water in each country is very different. The company must also communicate and market differently in each context, based on the diversity of each culture. Jesus called Simon and Andrew, two fishermen, to become his disciples who make disciples in a way that made sense in their context: "*I will send you out to fish for people.*" You will need to do the same in your context.

That doesn't mean there isn't some kind of template or consistent standard for how we define a disciple. As each of us thinks about clearly defining what a disciple is and how one is made in our context, we want Jesus' words to guide how we develop our definition and process.

Let's consider the bookends of Jesus' calling in Matthew 4:19 and Jesus' final moments with his disciples in Matthew 28:17-20. The call to "Come, follow me ... and I will send you out to fish for people" after following Jesus for more than three years is concluded with these words: "And when they [the 11 disciples] saw him, they worshiped him; but some doubted. Then Jesus came to them and said, 'All authority in heaven and on earth has been given to me. Therefore go and make disciples of all nations, baptizing them in the name of the Father and of the Son and of the Holy Spirit, teaching them to obey everything I have commanded you. And surely I am with you always, to the very end of the age'" (NIV).

We can discern from these verses (and many other verses as well) three key parts to the definition of a disciple. The definition must be: 1) relational, 2) transformational, and 3) commissional.

Relational

Disciple-making is a relational activity. When a rabbi called disciples to himself, he was calling them to follow his way of living closely. The ancient Jewish blessing captures this concept well: *May you be covered in the dust of your rabbi.* To be a disciple of a rabbi required that you follow him closely—so closely that you would get covered by the dust of his sandals. Jesus called the disciples to follow him, to do life together with him, and in the end, they worshiped him. Later, after Jesus ascended to heaven, Peter and John were brought before the religious leaders and teachers for trial. When the leaders saw the courage of Peter and John, realizing they were unschooled, ordinary men, the leaders were astonished and recognized that Peter and John had been *with Jesus.*

To be a disciple of Jesus is to be with Jesus. Jesus makes this so clear in John 15:5, "I am the vine; you are the branches. If you remain in me and I in you, you will bear much fruit; apart from me you can do nothing." Jesus calls us to relationship that is constant and dependent. He calls us to a relational intimacy and to a dependency that looks to him for the ability to live an abundant, fruitful life. Matthew records Jesus telling his disciples that he has all authority in heaven and on earth and that he will be *with* them always. So being a disciple of Jesus is about submission to Jesus as lord and attaching to Jesus as our empowering companion.

Dallas Willard has written and spoken extensively on the nature of spiritual formation, and his work is a huge gift to the Church. However, in all his years, he witnessed many devout Christians read his books, follow his counsel, and faithfully engage in spiritual practices and exercises yet not experience much transformation into Christlike maturity. In his book *Renovated,* Jim Wilder shares conversations he had with Dallas

Willard about what might be missing in our attempts to help people become more like Jesus.

In one conversation, with only weeks to live and with tears in his eyes, Dallas said to Jim, "What I have learned in this last year is more important than what I learned in the rest of my life. But I have no time to write about it. You need to write about this." And with mounting passion Dallas stated, "I know of no soteriology (doctrine of salvation) based on forming a new attachment with God."[1] Knowledge about God and right beliefs about God—if they are divorced from true attachment love from and with God—will not bring lasting transformation. *Renovated* explores how attachment love from and with God is what brings true transformation.

This is what Jesus is saying in John 15 when he tells his disciples they must abide in him and he in them if they are to be fruitful. He prays to God the Father with this same thought in John 17:3 when he says, "This is eternal life: that they know you, the only true God, and Jesus Christ, whom you have sent." This word know is not merely pertaining to having ideas about God and Jesus Christ. It means to be intimately and relationally connected to them. In fact, Jesus further clarifies this later in his prayer in John 17:20-21 as he prays for all of us who will believe in him: "My prayer is not for them alone. I pray also for those who will believe in me through their message, that all of them may be one, Father, just as you are in me and I am in you. May they also be in us so that the world may believe that you have sent me." Paul writes a similar message to the church in Colossae when he says, "To them God has chosen to make known among the Gentiles the glorious riches of this mystery, which is Christ in you, the hope of glory. He is the one we proclaim, admonishing and teaching everyone with all wisdom, so that we may present everyone fully mature in Christ" (Colossians 1:27-28). The maturity Paul describes requires an intimate relationship with Jesus.

Jesus, Paul, Dallas, and Jim are all saying the same thing. You will never grow up into Christlike maturity unless you are lovingly attached in an intimate relationship with God the Father and Jesus the Son through the powerful presence and work of the Spirit.

Our definition of a disciple of Jesus must include this relationship. And so must our practices, as we will see. If the beliefs, teaching, and practices that we engage in (and call others to engage in) do not bring about attachment love from and with God, we are nothing. For God is love, and without love, as Paul instructs the Corinthian church, we have nothing and we are nothing.[2]

Transformational

Relational attachment from and with Jesus will bring about transformation that looks like Jesus. When he calls his first disciples, Jesus promises that if they follow him and be with him, he will *make* them into something new. Then, in his final words, he commands his disciples—relying on his power and presence—to go and make disciples. He continues by instructing them to baptize new disciples in (or into) the name of the Father, the name of the Son, and the name of the Holy Spirit. To baptize means to immerse into, so as to take on the nature or identity of the immersion.[3]

For example, in those days you would baptize a piece of fabric in red dye, and the fabric would become red. One would then say that the fabric had been baptized in red and therefore into red. It had taken on the very substance of what it was baptized into. This concept of baptism was representative of a new identity. To be baptized in (and into) the name of Father, Son, and Holy Spirit is a visible picture of a new reality. Your new baptismal identity is a **child of God** the Father, born again by the Spirit; **a servant** of King Jesus and an extension of his servant-like rule and reign on the earth; and **a sent one**, empowered by the Holy Spirit to be a witness to the world of Jesus' life, death, and resurrection. A disciple of Jesus is a changed person with an entirely new nature and identity, which leads to an entirely new way of living. Paul says in 2 Corinthians 5:17, "Therefore, if anyone is in Christ, the new creation has come. The old has gone, the new is here!"

One of the most profound truths of the Christian faith is that we are free from the world's system that has trained us to believe that what we do is who we are—that our activity leads to our identity. This is the empty and powerless religion of our world. The heart of the Christian faith is that we are who we are, not because of what we have done, but because of what God in Christ Jesus has done for us and is doing in us and through us. If our faith is in Jesus and all that he accomplished for us through his life, death, and resurrection, then our lives are in him as well. Our lives are hidden with Christ in God,[4] and we become co-heirs of Christ.[5] All that he is and all that he has done and is doing define all that we are.

Paul continues this thought of being a new creation in Christ in 2 Corinthians 5:21, saying, "God made him who had no sin to be sin for us, so that in him we might become the righteousness of God." We went from an identity of being sinners to being righteous. We went from dead to alive,[6] from enemy of God[7] to child of God.[8]

As a new creation, a disciple is called to not only know their new identity but to actively put off the old and put on the new, which is another way of saying to live out who you really are now. Paul instructs the church in Ephesus with these words: "I tell you this, and insist on it in the Lord, that you must no longer live as the Gentiles [not yet disciples of Jesus] do, in the futility of their thinking. They are darkened in their understanding and separated from the life of God [notice the detachment here] because of the ignorance that is in them due to the hardening of their hearts. Having lost all sensitivity, they have given themselves up to sensuality so as to indulge in every kind of impurity, and they are full of greed. That, however, is not the way of life you learned when you heard about Christ and were taught in him in accordance with the truth that is in Jesus, to put off your old self, which is being corrupted by its deceitful desires; to be made new in the attitude of your minds; and to put on the new self, created to be like God in true righteousness and holiness" (Ephesians 4:17-24).

Disciples of Jesus are new people, but they can still live like they are not[9]. Our old selves were alienated from the life of God—but now we are new, and we have access to the very life of God in Jesus Christ. That is what eternal life is. Eternal life is not just life after death. Eternal life is a whole new kind of living made possible now by the very life of God in you. And this new life lines up with a new self that is created after the likeness of God in true righteousness and holiness. We are new, but we also need to learn to live in this new way.

A key part of being a disciple of Jesus is putting off the old and walking in the new, becoming more and more like Jesus in our feelings, thoughts, words, and actions. This was the desire of disciples in Jesus' day. They wanted to be with their rabbi so they could become like the rabbi. Being with Jesus leads to becoming like Jesus. Then we are able to do the things Jesus did and is still doing.

Commissional

Jesus told his disciples he would show them how to fish for people. Then later he commanded them to make disciples, baptizing them into their new identity, teaching them to obey all that he commanded them, promising that he would be with them the entire time. Dallas Willard encouraged readers to ask their pastors, "What is your plan for teaching our people to do everything Christ commanded?" Our definition of a disciple *must* include the aspect of doing what Jesus commanded—and, I would add, doing it through Jesus' powerful presence at work in us and through us.

When my wife and I called a small group of disciples to join us in starting a new church in Tacoma, Washington, we wanted the goal to be that every disciple of Jesus could make disciples of Jesus who obey all that Jesus commanded. Sadly, in far too many cases, Christians believe that disciple-making disciples are the ninjas of Christianity, not the norm.[10] This was never Jesus' plan.

With this goal in mind, we recognized that we would need to take a close look at all that Jesus commanded his disciples to do. As we considered everything Jesus commanded, we made a list. Then we set out to train the new disciples to obey every command of Jesus. We knew it was not sufficient just to tell them what to do. Our most effective disciple-making over the years always included show and tell. We needed to both teach *and* demonstrate to help people learn in real time how to obey Jesus' commands. So, with each of Jesus' commands, we either tried to create real-life learning scenarios or prayed that Jesus would provide them.

One of the opportunities Jesus gave us centered on his command to heal the sick.[11] A brother of one of our core group members was dying of cancer. He had a brain tumor and was given very little time to live. His sister called and asked if we could pray for his healing. I said yes, we could, but I wanted him to come to our weekly meal and training time a little later so that I could take the time to teach our group about healing before he arrived. His dad, who was not yet a Christian, decided to show up early. He listened in as I walked through the biblical passages that teach us about healing. The brother, who had walked away from Jesus, arrived after the teaching time, and we started by asking what he wanted. He said he wanted to be healed. We then asked if he had any sin he wanted to confess. He got on his knees, without us directing him, and began to confess his sin and profess his faith in Jesus. We proceeded to pray for his healing.

A few weeks later, we were informed that he had been healed! However, he was still pretty weak and needed help around the house. So we went and practiced another of Jesus' commands—serving those in need. I ended up power washing his driveway and sidewalk with his father. His father was curious as to why we were doing all of this for his son, so I shared about God's love for us in Jesus and how we serve others because Jesus has served us.

In that scenario, we were able to show *and* tell three of Jesus' commands to the small group of Jesus-followers we were responsible for: heal the sick, serve those in need, proclaim the gospel. That is what teaching disciples to obey Jesus' commands looks like. This can't happen in a classroom. It happens in real life.

And, to be clear, Jesus doesn't command us to do this on our own, but with him. Jesus calls his disciples to be on his mission, doing what he is doing with him as he is doing it in us and through us. The Great Commission is not a mission we are sent on by Jesus to do for Jesus. The "Great Co-Mission" is about joining Jesus on his mission in the world.

A disciple is one who is with Jesus, being transformed by Jesus, and doing what Jesus is doing in the world.

Putting It Together

As you think about how you define a disciple, make sure your definition is relational, transformational, and commissional. Some examples of how a disciple could be defined are:

- A disciple of Jesus is committed to be with Jesus, become like Jesus, and do what Jesus did and is doing.
- A disciple of Jesus worships Jesus, is being changed by Jesus, and obeys everything Jesus commands.
- A disciple of Jesus follows Jesus, is transformed by Jesus, and joins Jesus on mission in the world.

Some choose to capture this in identity language. For instance:

- A disciple is a child of God who loves others like family, a servant of Jesus who serves others like Jesus served them, and a missionary sent and empowered by the Spirit to show and share Jesus.

How about you? How do you define who a disciple is, and how do you sense Jesus is inviting you to join him in making disciples who make disciples?

NOTES

1. Quoted from page 1 of Jim Wilder's book *Renovated: God, Dallas Willard and the Church That Transforms*. Jim includes several of Dallas Willard's lectures given at the Heart and Soul Conference. In these lectures, Dallas addresses the relationship of spiritual maturity to emotional maturity.

2. 1 Corinthians 13:1-3

3. For more on baptismal identity consider this animated description from Saturate resources: https://saturatetheworld.com/resource/church-is-more/baptismal-identity/ You might also be interested in reading *Saturate—Making Disciples in the Everyday Stuff of Life*, by Jeff Vanderstelt, which goes into much greater detail about how we form familial communities on mission in light of our baptismal identity.

4. Colossians 3:3

5. Romans 8:17

6. Ephesians 2:4

7. Romans 5:8; Ephesians 2:3

8. Romans 8:14-17

9. This is what Paul describes more extensively in Romans 7-8. I find that this is a very confusing reality for many Christians. Some regularly question their salvation because they believe that if they struggle in the way Paul describes in Romans 7, they either are not Christians or they have lost their salvation. I often encourage people in this struggle that the fact that they are struggling is a good sign. They want to do what is good and right even though they struggle to always do it. In most cases, this is both evidence that they are saved (they have a new heart that wants to do what God wants) and that they are aware they need to experience the ongoing salvation of Jesus (being saved like Paul describes in 1 Corinthians 15:1-2).

10. I was once sharing at a conference with a very well-known and influential pastor during a Q&A session about disciple-making. This particular pastor shared that I primarily worked with ninja Christians, the few who actually were committed to making disciples. He continued saying that he doesn't believe most Christians will ever commit to and be able to make disciples, so his primary job was to teach them and to help them connect in community. Sadly, though most pastors will never say it this clearly, far too many believe the same thing. Because of this, so few Christians believe Jesus actually intended the Great Commission to be carried out by all Christians.

11. Dandelion Resources is a wonderfully helpful training ministry that equips the Church to walk in naturally supernatural ways. Training disciples to pray for healing is one of the things they are very effective at training Christians

CHAPTER TWO
The Process of Making Disciples

Once you have a definition of a disciple, you will need to think through the process of making disciples. Far too often, churches and ministries create moments for decisions but fail to create pathways for making disciples. If we fail to connect decision-making moments to disciple-making processes, we unnecessarily create immature deciders instead of mature disciples. Making disciples who know how to be with Jesus, become like Jesus, and do what Jesus did (and is doing) is not a one-moment decision but an ongoing process.

One of the ways we've helped churches develop a disciple-making process is by thinking of disciple-making work like a relational journey. We start by helping them clarify their destination: How do they define a mature disciple? Then we help them map out the journey a person will take to move from a non-believer to a new believer to a mature disciple of Jesus who makes disciples. Some call this journey a "disciple-making pathway." Disciple-making is really like spiritual parenting. If we use familial language, we can identify five key stages in the disciple-making pathway: 1) spiritually dead; 2) spiritual infant; 3) spiritual child; 4) spiritual young adult; and 5) spiritual parent.[1]

Spiritually Dead

Paul reminds the church in Ephesus of who they used to be: "You were dead in your transgressions and sins, in which you used to live."[2] We were all once spiritually dead. The word *death* in Hebrew means "separated." When Paul says in Romans 6:23 "the wages of sin is death, but the gift of God is eternal life in Christ Jesus our Lord," he is saying that "the result of sin is spiritual and relational separation (death) from God, others, and self; but God in Christ Jesus freely gives us a new spiritual relationship (eternal life) with God, others, and self."

As we think about getting back to disciple-making and designing a process for making disciples, we must recognize that it starts with being around people who are spiritually dead—people disconnected from God and from God's redeeming people, the Church.

Paul reminds the Church in Ephesus, "You were dead (separated) in your transgressions and sins. … But because of his great love for us, God, who is rich in mercy, made us alive with (notice the relational nature) Christ even when we were dead in transgressions—it is by grace you have been saved. And God raised us up with Christ and seated us with him in the heavenly realms in Christ Jesus" (Ephesians 2:2-6). It was through a loving relationship that these Jesus-followers were brought to life-giving faith in him. Paul says it another way in verses 12-13: "Remember that you were at that time *separate* from

Christ, excluded from citizenship in Israel and foreigners to the covenants of the promise, without hope and without God in the world. But now in Christ Jesus you who once were far away have been brought near by the blood of Christ." Paul continues to describe how God in Jesus Christ removed every barrier so that the Gentiles would be welcomed into the family of God and become true citizens with the saints and fellow members of God's household.

Paul doesn't want them to forget their heritage—partly because he wants them to live out their true unity in the faith and give no opportunity for division. However, Paul also wants them to recognize that the love they have experienced and the relational reconciliation they have received is to be extended to others who are still spiritually dead (separated from God and his family).[3] There are many others who have yet to experience the rich-in-mercy, life-saving love of God in Christ Jesus, and it is through God's people on mission in the world in loving relationship with the spiritually dead that they will come to be saved.

So, does your disciple-making pathway put disciples of Jesus in ongoing, consistent, loving relationships with those who have yet to be saved? And do those who know Jesus remember who they were before Jesus? Do they remember their way of living? Do they extend the same grace they received? Those who are spiritually dead—disconnected from the life and power of God to live a different life—should not be expected to live like those who are spiritually alive. God was rich in mercy toward us so that we can be full of mercy toward others.

I'm regularly amazed at how judgmental we Christians can be toward those who don't yet have a relationship with God.

Why would we expect them to live like Jesus when they don't yet have a relationship with him? We reveal our own misunderstanding of the Christian faith when we call people to live like Jesus who are not yet connected to him. It shows we think being a Christian is about *our own efforts* to be righteous and not about the power of Christ in us to enable us to live a new life.

How do we establish these relationships? We start by creating safe and hospitable places for non-Christians to be who they really are without expecting them to change on their own. This is the heart of hospitality—creating a safe place for the stranger or outsider to be at home with us just as they are.[4] There is a reason this is a requirement for church leaders. They are called to set an example of hospitality for the whole church so that every disciple is equipped to create a similar space. And then, while these new friends are feeling safe and at home in our presence, we love them like we are loved by our Heavenly Father. We serve them like we were served by King Jesus. We pray for them to experience the loving mercy of our God, and we are prepared to share with them the gospel that can give them new life.

And when they truly hear the gospel and believe in Jesus Christ, they too will be saved and experience a new birth. They will be reconnected to God through Jesus by the Spirit, empowering them to live a new life in the new family of God they are now a part of.

Spiritual Infant

The second stage begins once someone has experienced regeneration, what Jesus referred to as being "born again" by the Spirit.[5] Peter reminds us that we all were once like newborn infants in the faith who should long for pure spiritual milk so that by it we might grow up into salvation.[6] The spiritual infant is spiritually weak and very vulnerable. They are ignorant of the basic truths of the faith. They lack spiritual discernment and can easily be confused or deceived. Paul, when addressing the church in Corinth, refers to many of the people there as infants in Christ because they were still living in the old human way of the flesh.[7]

One of the things that greatly concerns me in the church is our drive to produce spiritual babies with little or no concern for helping them grow up into maturity. If we only concern ourselves with seeing new people come to faith but not with establishing those same people in their faith, we are just creating spiritual orphans who gather together regularly in a parentless orphanage. We have lots of spiritual babies with few to no spiritual parents to raise them.

According to Jesus, the first thing we do with spiritual newborns is establish them in the faith through baptism. Whenever we baptize new believers, we instruct them in the basics. We inform them that baptism is a physical expression of a spiritual reality. As they go underwater, their old life is buried with Christ in his burial, and they are raised with Christ in his resurrection to new life. This new life comes with a new identity. In most of our Soma Churches, we explain their new identity like this:

> We are baptizing you into the name of the Father because you are now a child of God who belongs to the Family of God. And as the children of God, we

are called to imitate God as beloved children who love others like we have been loved by God.

We are baptizing you into the name of the Son because you are now a servant of Jesus the King, who came not to be served but to serve and give his life as a ransom for you. As a servant of Jesus, serve others as your act of worship toward Jesus.

We are baptizing you into the name of the Spirit because you are now a missionary of Jesus, sent with the power and presence of the same Spirit that empowered Jesus to do everything he did on his mission from the Father.

Like newborn babies need milk, these spiritual babies need spiritual milk.[8] What does this mean? Like a mother of a newborn must eat and digest food and then give it to her child in the form of milk, the newborn Christian needs someone else to feed them the basic nutrients for spiritual growth. The writer of Hebrews says we must teach them the basic truths about God and how to discern what is right and wrong.[9] In this early stage of making disciples, a lot more intentional time together in God's Word and prayer is necessary. We need to read God's Word with them and teach them how to pray by praying together, not just telling them to pray on their own. The practice of prayer must include spoken prayer and listening prayer (some call this breathing in and breathing out prayer).

At this stage, we also help them learn to spiritually speak. Just like little children learn how to speak, we need to teach spiritual infants to give voice to what is going on inside of them. We need confessional communities that create safe places for spiritual infants to practice regular confession. We need to train them to confess out loud what is going on inside. This includes confessing their feelings, thoughts, beliefs, desires, and needs. The Psalms are a great training tool to teach spiritual infants to write and express themselves to God in prayer and to others through confession. And disciple-making communities (spiritual families) need to foster space for people to grow in sharing their true selves through regular confession.

If the spiritual newborns don't yet know the overarching Story of God in the Bible, you will want to ground them in it. We are all formed and shaped by story, and a key part of human development is story-work. For many, the dominant story they live with is the broken family system narrative in which they grew up. In order to walk in their new creation identity that they received through Jesus, spiritual infants need to learn the larger Story of God that brings healing and redemption to their story of origin, and also enables them to see that they are part of a much bigger and better story which gives their life great significance and direction.

Many groups have developed means to share the whole redemptive arc of the Bible in oral form.[10] *The Jesus Storybook Bible* by Sally Lloyd Jones is also a very helpful tool, regardless of the actual age of the person reading it. These and other practices like silence, solitude, sabbath, fasting, etc. are meant to train the new disciple in the practice of abiding in Christ. They will not grow up in the faith if this doesn't happen. Apart from Jesus (true attachment to Jesus), they can do nothing.[11]

They also need to learn to tell their own story with Jesus as the hero. One doesn't have to be mature in the faith to share their testimony. As soon as a person comes to new life in Jesus, they have a powerful story to tell—the story of how Jesus changed them. We need to equip every new believer to share their story.[12]

Spiritual Child

Jesus said that after baptizing new believers, we are to teach them to obey everything he commanded them. As we teach them his commands, we need to properly ground the commands in the person and work of God in Jesus Christ so that they don't just adopt a new moral or legal code, leading them to depend on the flesh to attain their own righteousness. Over the years I have found it helpful to establish new believers in a gospel paradigm using Five Key Questions:[13]

1. Who is God?
2. What has God done—most fully in Christ?
3. Who are we?
4. What do we do?
5. How do we do it?

The first three questions are indicatives—things that are true no matter what I do. The last two are imperatives—what I do because of what is true.

For instance, the command to love our enemies and pray for those who persecute us (imperative) is grounded in the truths that:

1. God is love. (Who is God?)
2. God loved us through Christ while we were still enemies, and Jesus also prayed for us from the cross. (What has God done?)
3. We, who were enemies, are now the Beloved. (Who are we?)

Leading us to:

4. Love our enemies and pray for those who persecute us, like Jesus did for us. (What do we do?)

And in light of my context:

5. The Spirit empowers me to love my co-worker by being patient and gracious, forgiving him for making disrespectful comments about me. (How do we do it?)

If you look closely at the questions, you will see the core themes of biblical training:

1. Who is God? (theology—study of God)
2. What has God done—most fully in Christ? (Christology—study of Christ/salvation)
3. Who are we? (Ecclesiology—study of the Church)
4. What do we do? (Missiology—mission of the Church)
5. How do we do it? (Contextualization—applied theology, Christology, ecclesiology, and missiology to a particular person in a particular time and a particular place)

Like children, new believers can't do this on their own. They will need to be established in community with older disciples of Jesus around them, teaching and training them in the way of Jesus and correcting and rebuking them when necessary.[14]

It is in community with older disciples that they learn to practice the "one anothers."[15] Regular and consistent time in community around feasting, learning, praying, and serving provide the context to grow up in love. Paul reminded Timothy that the goal of his instruction was love from a pure heart, a good conscience, and a sincere faith.[16] Jesus made it clear that all the commandments hang on love for God and loving others as yourself.[17] Life in community provides ample opportunities to love one another, pray for one another, forgive one another, bear one another's burdens, rejoice with one another, and weep with one another. Similar to physical development, this stage of our spiritual development is all about relationships. Jesus said the world would know we are his disciples by our love for one another.

Spiritual Young Adult

At this stage, spiritual parents need to create spaces and opportunities for disciples to begin to discover and develop their spiritual gifts and engage in practical ministry experiences with clear feedback loops for ongoing development. That is what Jesus did. Jesus sent his disciples out in pairs to practice everything he had demonstrated and taught. When they returned, he created space to reflect on what they experienced, and then he gave additional training and correction where needed. A good way to think about this stage is apprenticeship.

An unfortunate reality in far too many churches is that the invitation to serve is often limited to the activities that can be done by spiritual children, and the other activities that require greater maturity are only done by spiritual parents. Many of these churches wonder why they have very few people able to teach others or lead multiplying ministries, but there are often very few opportunities for spiritual young adults to grow up into spiritual parenthood. This leaves an obvious gap in the disciple-making pathway.

One of the reasons this happens is because some churches or ministries have a sort of fraternal order of leadership. Like a sorority or fraternity that continues to raise the demands on new pledges who want to enter, many church leaders raise the entry bar on apprentice leadership opportunities in the church. Sadly, the only people given the opportunity are middle-aged and above. These same churches or ministries eventually age out and die because they have no means of raising up future generations.

We need to create safe and healthy development cultures for disciples to grow into spiritual parents. Development cultures create space to share leadership. When churches and ministries model shared leadership at all levels, disciples know there is space for them as well. A development culture should also create ongoing practical experiences for development in various areas. Think about raising young adult children. Every good parent works hard to give their young adults practical experience in everything they will need to do to start and lead their own family someday. With that, there must be a gracious culture where there is freedom to fail. No one develops by doing everything right. We learn and grow through failure. And, we must intentionally create vacuums for people to step into. Spiritual parents need to get out of the way to make room for spiritual young adults to step up.

Spiritual Parent

Spiritual parenting consists of making disciples and creating disciple-making environments and pathways. Physically healthy parents make babies, train up children, prepare young adults, and then bless those young adults to lead their own homes and families someday. The same is true for spiritual parents.

The writer of Hebrews rebukes his listeners, saying, "Though by this time you ought to be teachers, you need someone to teach you the elementary truths of God's word all over again. You need milk, not solid food!" (Hebrews 5:12). I've heard many Christians say something like, "We choose to come to this church because this church feeds us solid food, not milk like our past church." This is a clear misunderstanding of this passage and what spiritual maturity is. What they are actually saying is, "We choose this church because they serve us a different kind of milk than the last one." Remember, milk is the result of someone else eating solid food and feeding you liquid food from it. Anyone who still needs someone to study the Word and make it easy to digest for them is still an infant, according to Scripture. The mature eat solid food themselves and can feed others milk from what they have digested. In other words, they can learn on their own and teach others the truth of God themselves. They no longer need someone to teach them.[18]

Spiritual parents make disciples who create disciple-making environments that raise up spiritual children to become spiritual parents themselves. One of the greatest weaknesses of the present Church is that we have applauded creating spaces where people are continually in need of a few to do all the ministry for the many, leading to perpetual infancy of Christians.

What if the new norm and expected metric in the Church was that every believer is trained up to be a spiritual parent? That is what Paul calls the Ephesian church to in Ephesians 4:11-16: "And he gave some to be apostles, some prophets, some evangelists, some shepherds and teachers, to equip the saints for the work of ministry, to build up the body of Christ, until we all reach unity in the faith and in the knowledge of God's Son, growing into maturity with a stature measured by Christ's fullness. Then we will no longer be little children, tossed by the waves and blown around by every wind of teaching, by human cunning with cleverness in the techniques of deceit. But speaking the truth in love, let us grow up in every way into him who is the head - Christ. From him the whole body, fitted and knit together by every supporting ligament, promotes the growth of the body for building itself up in love by the proper working of each individual part."

That is what the next shift is all about: a shift from informing to equipping.

NOTES

1. Jim Putman puts this together in his stages of growth chart: https://jimputman.com/wp-content/uploads/2018/06/The-5-Stages-Of-Spiritual-Growth-1.pdf

2. Ephesians 2:1-2

3. Also consider 2 Corinthians 5:16-20 where Paul reminds believers that we who have been reconciled with God are now given the ministry of reconciliation, calling us to share the message of reconciliation with the world as his ambassadors.

4. *The Gospel Comes with a House Key: Practicing Radically Ordinary Hospitality in Our Post-Christian World*, by Rosaria Butterfield is a very helpful book on hospitality.

5. John 3:1-8

6. 1 Peter 2:2

7. 1 Corinthians 3:1

8. 1 Peter 2:2

9. Hebrews 5:11-14

10. Saturate has created several helpful tools for telling the overarching story of the Bible. You can go to saturatetheworld.com and look up "Story of God" and "Story-formed Way" to find more resources.

11. John 15:5

12. Saturate provides many resources for how to share your story with Jesus as the hero. Go to saturatetheworld.com and search for "Share Your Story."

13. *Gospel Fluency: Speaking the Truths of Jesus Into the Everyday Stuff of Life* by Jeff Vanderstelt and *The Gospel Fluency Handbook* by Jeff Vanderstelt and Ben Connelly works this out in greater detail.

14. 2 Timothy 3:16-17

15. There are 94 verses in the New Testament that contain 100 commands for us to do to "one another."

16. 1 Timothy 1:5

17. Matthew 22:37-40

18. This doesn't mean it is wrong to sit under good teaching. People of all ages and spiritual maturity levels can benefit from others teaching God's Word. However, mature Christians are no longer primarily dependent upon someone else digesting and regurgitating God's Word for them. They can feed themselves if they are mature.

CHAPTER THREE

Building a Disciple-Making Pathway

After two chapters on each shift, we will provide a guided process for you and your team to develop your own working plan. The shift from reaching people to making disciples who make disciples requires that we define who a disciple is and develop a process that takes a person through a disciple-making pathway.

DEFINITION OF DISCIPLE

Take some time to brainstorm together with your team the key ideas and words that best capture how you might define a disciple. Remember to keep in mind the relational (with), transformational (like), and commissional (do) aspects.

Brainstorm Definition Ideas:

Definition of a Disciple:

DISCIPLE-MAKING PATHWAY

The disciple-making pathway includes reaching people who are not yet spiritually alive in Christ, leading them to faith in Jesus Christ through a hospitable missional life that is committed to showing and sharing Jesus, establishing new followers of Jesus in their faith, helping them grow up into maturity, and then preparing and sending them to become spiritual parents who start and lead new spiritual families themselves. Some churches decide to write their pathway for how spiritual parents will begin new spiritual families. Others decide to write their pathway starting with the person who is not yet alive in Christ. And some put the two together. The Kansas City Underground combines them.[1] Saturate has also created video and downloadable resources to help you build your own disciple-making pathway.[2]

Pathway Example

1. **PRAYER AND FASTING**—Start with prayer and fasting to discern who God is calling you to love, serve, and share Jesus with. (This requires training people to listen to God in prayer and practice discerning prayer together.)

2. **ENGAGE IN B.L.E.S.S. PRACTICES**—Begin praying for the people; Listen to their stories; Eat meals together; Serve their needs; Share your story with Jesus as the hero. (This requires training people to B.L.E.S.S. others.)

3. **SPIRITUAL CONVERSATIONS**—Move from casual conversations to spiritual conversations to Jesus conversations. (This requires training people to become gospel fluent.)[3]

4. **INTRODUCE BIBLICAL TRUTH**—When ready, invite people to go through Story-Formed Way[4] or engage in a Discovery Bible Study. (This requires training people in how to lead either.)

5. **SURRENDER TO JESUS**—Lead people, when ready, to surrender their lives to Jesus in prayer.

6. **BAPTISM**—Baptize new believers and establish them in their new baptismal identity.

7. **THE BASICS**—Equip new believers to relationally attach to God through reading or listening to the Bible and through prayer.

8. **RELATIONAL SPACES**—Teach growing believers to engage in key relational spaces for their own development.

9. **GIFTEDNESS**—Help them identify who they are as a gift, what skills they've been given as gifts, and how to engage in the spiritual manifestation gifts.

10. **PRAYER AND FASTING**—When ready, engage once again in prayer and fasting to discern who God may be calling them to love, serve, and share Jesus with.

Building Your Pathway

Which practices will mature disciples need to be trained in to reach people who are not yet followers of Jesus (i.e. hospitality, sharing personal story, Discovery Bible Study, etc.)?

- Personal relationship w/ God.
- Quiet time w/ God — Just being w/ Him in silence
-

What is the general order for how you will lead people to start relationships, build trust, share the gospel, establish in the faith, build up to maturity, and prepare and send to new mission fields?

Preparing for the Mission

• prayer, people peaking into life.

Activities for <u>Starting Relationships</u>

✴ Trusting Holy Spirit. Bring someone w/ you to gym —

Engaging in Spiritual Conversations

• whats your experience w/ Jesus?
• Ask ppl if they want prayer.

Starting and Establishing in the Faith

Strengthening in the Faith

• we are all called to ministry where God has put us, live, work, and play. · ·

Preparing for Mission

Discerning and Sending on Mission

* These experiences are not the character of God.

· open mouth and let Holy Spirit take over — you cannot make a disciple unless yeilded to the Spirit.

(· Eph 4:4-8) Ps 68:18

· That Jesus may be known through me...
· Be who God called you to be...
· What have you been given as a gift to Build God's Kingdom? — what spiritual gift

— Are you doing what God has called you to do?
— Are teaching others?
· Shepherd / teacher?

NOTES

1. You can learn more about the Kansas City Underground's Missionary Pathway here: https://kcunderground.org

2. Saturate has created a video series and a PDF to help you design your own pathway. You can find both at saturatetheworld.com. https://saturatetheworld.com/2022/05/16/a-pathway-for-discipleship/

3. For more resources on gospel fluency go to: https://saturatetheworld.com/growing-in-gospel-fluency For a free chapter from my book on Gospel Fluency go to: https://saturatetheworld.com/resource/gospel-fluency-book/

4. Saturate has resources for walking through the narrative arc of Scripture for adults and kids. Check out the "Story-Formed Way" and "Story of God for Kids" available with a Saturate membership: https://saturatetheworld.com/membership

SHIFT #2

FROM INFORMING TO EQUIPPING

FROM INFORMING TO EQUIPPING

One of the biggest reasons we don't see a movement of disciple-making disciples is because the few are doing the work of the many. We've bought into this false notion that some Christians are called to ministry, and the rest are not. As a result, the few who believe they are called take on the burden of doing all the work, while the majority watch and applaud. It's not sustainable, and it doesn't accomplish the plan the Lord has in mind for his Church. God has called every Christian into ministry, and it is the job of the Church to equip every follower of Jesus for the work of ministry.

We also have a deficiency of training. We largely are being trained by shepherds and teachers, but we have little to no equipping being done by apostles, prophets, and evangelists as Paul instructed the Church to include (Ephesians 4:11-12). As a result, most expressions of church look like teaching centers and care groups. We need a much more full and diverse expression of Jesus displayed through his body.

Another reason we don't see a disciple-making movement is because we have falsely believed that informing equals equipping. We presently have more access to information than at any other time in history. You can get information about anything at any moment. But information without heart transformation leads to spiritual deformation. Knowing more information is not enough. We need to shift from informing to equipping. We need to equip people in much more holistic ways that are D.E.E.P.E.R. than just informing them. God has not given some of us to the Church to dispense information. God has given all of us to the Church to holistically equip each other for ministry that looks like the fullness of Jesus.

CHAPTER FOUR

Equipping God's People

If we are going to make a shift from informing to equipping, we are going to have to embrace the calling to see every disciple of Jesus set free and empowered to be a gift and to equip others as gifts.

He Gave People Gifts

Ephesians 4:7-8 (CSB) says, "Now grace was given to each one of us according to the measure of Christ's gift. For it says: *When he ascended on high, he took the captives captive; he gave gifts to people.*" This quote from Psalm 68:18 is a reference to God's deliverance of his people from slavery in Egypt. However, a significant change took place from the time the original Psalm was written to the writing of this letter to the Ephesians. Before God delivered his people from slavery in Egypt, he worked to grant favor to the Israelites so that when they asked their neighbors for silver and gold, the Egyptians gave it to them. Therefore, the Israelites left Egypt with plenty of provisions. Psalm 68:18

informs the reader that the Lord received gifts from this plunder. However, in Ephesians 4:8, we read that the Lord is now giving gifts to humans. And what are these gifts? Ephesians 4:11 says, "And he gave some to be apostles, some prophets, some evangelists, some shepherds and teachers." The gifts Christ gives to the world are *people*.

Whenever I teach about spiritual gifts, I describe how God has given three kinds of gifts to build up the body of Christ. In this passage we see that God gives *people* as gifts: apostles, prophets, evangelists, shepherds, and teachers. In other passages like Romans 12:6-8, we see that God gives *skill* gifts to people—like serving, teaching, giving, encouraging, leading, and showing mercy. (This list is an example of some of the skill gifts, not an exhaustive list of every skill gift.) And lastly there are the *manifestation* gifts that we read about in 1 Corinthians 12:7-10, when Paul says, "Now to each one the manifestation of the Spirit is given for the common good." He then describes these manifestations as a message of wisdom, a message of knowledge, faith, healing, the working of miracles, prophecy, the ability to distinguish between spirits, tongues, and the interpretation of tongues. In each case Paul makes it clear that these are brought about by the Spirit. So, it seems these manifestation gifts are given *by the Spirit* at any time for the need of the moment.

In summary, God gives you *as* a gift (people gifts). God gives *you* gifts (skill gifts). And God gives you manifestations of the Spirit to *gift* you for the moment (manifestation gifts). If you were to compare this to a tradesperson, you might think of a carpenter, electrician, or plumber (people) with different tools on their tool belts (skills), and power cords or batteries to empower their work (manifestation). The analogy breaks down a bit at the end there. But thinking about gifts this way can be far more helpful than just lumping all the gifts into one big category.

Now, why are the gifts given? For the good of the body, to edify, to build up, and to equip for ministry. In his letter to the church in Ephesus, Paul is clear that these people gifts were previously in captivity. They were not free to be given to equip the Church for ministry. Jesus came to set every one of us free to be given as gifts for the building up of the Church. In Ephesians 4:12-14 , Paul goes on to describe the aim of Jesus' generosity as being "to equip the saints for the work of ministry, for building up the body of Christ, until we all attain to the unity of the faith and of the knowledge of the Son of God, to mature manhood, to the measure of the stature of the fullness of Christ, so that we may no longer be children, tossed to and fro by the waves and carried about by every wind of doctrine, by human cunning, by craftiness in deceitful schemes."

The aim of Jesus' generosity is to equip saints—every believer in Jesus—for the work of ministry. The word for *ministry* could also be translated *service*. Unfortunately, many people read this passage and think only of ministry as the formal gatherings and events of the church (like children's ministry, youth ministry, worship ministry, etc.). Paul's intent is for us to understand ministry as any act of service that represents what Jesus is like. This could be at work, in our neighborhood, with our friends or family, at school, in our places of recreation, when we gather as the church, and more. Jesus set free the captives to equip God's people to serve others in everyday ways. And, as we do, in whatever expression Jesus gives us to serve, his aim is that the Church is built up into maturity.

Paul's description of maturity is a people who are unified in the faith, who have the full knowledge of who Jesus Christ is, and who, together, look like Jesus. Jesus' aim is that every believer is a mature expression of what he is like and is so unified with every other believer that the Church resembles the very person of Christ on earth. The goal is that, through his Church, Jesus fills every place (city, work, neighborhood, school, recreation, etc.) with his presence so that every person in every place has repeated opportunities to meet him everyday (see Ephesians 1:22-23).

I recently shared this with a group of marketplace leaders to encourage them to see their work as their ministry. I told them that Jesus set them free as gifts to give to others as a unique expression of who he is to the world. Afterward, a woman who worked in real estate told me she was so encouraged to realize she was an evangelist who never understood her calling. Now she was going to work with a new realization that, as she was sent to share good news, she would equip others as well.

This is the goal. If you want to see God, look at Jesus. If you want to see Jesus, look at the body of Christ, his Church—sent everywhere as ministers and equippers on mission everyday.

Diversity of Equipping

To achieve this goal, we not only need to devote ourselves to equipping every Christian, but we also need a diversity of equipping as well. One-on-one, one-to-ten, and one-to-one hundred forms of equipping will never lead to mature disciples who look like Jesus. New believers who are discipled by only one person will end up looking most like that one person, not the fullness of Christ. If the one person is a shepherd, her disciples will likely be very caring. If the one person is an evangelist, his disciples will become winsome storytellers and inviters. If the one person is a teacher, her disciples will look like skilled learners and teachers. If the one person is a prophet, his disciples will display and declare holiness and justice. If the one person is an apostle, his disciples will likely be very missional.

But Jesus isn't just one of these. Jesus is *all five*. Jesus is the true Apostle of our faith, sent to us by the Father, anointed, filled, and led by the Spirit as the ultimate missionary and founder of our faith.[1] He is also the true Prophet who announces that the time is fulfilled, and the Kingdom of God is brought about in fullness through him.[2] Jesus is the true Evangelist who not only proclaims the good news of the Kingdom, but also fulfills it as the Good News himself.[3] He is the true Shepherd who lays down his life for his sheep; pursues and finds those who are lost; protects, feeds, and guides those who are found; and brings healing to those who are wounded.[4] And Jesus is the true Teacher who is the way, the truth, and the life, revealing the truth of God in his life and his teaching.[5] He is the mystery of God revealed, and in him all the treasures of wisdom and knowledge are hidden.[6] If the Church is going to grow into the full knowledge of Christ and maturity as defined by the person and ministry of Christ, we need to be equipped with and ministered by all five people gifts (A.P.E.S.T. - apostle, prophet, evangelist, shepherd, teacher).

For far too long, the Church has been led and trained primarily by shepherds and teachers. We've seen some development in the last 30-40 years in valuing evangelists, though we need much more equipping from them for sure, but the apostles and prophets have been largely neglected. Some churches have done this because they believe these people gifts are no longer given to the Church (once the Scriptures were written and canonized).[7] I do not agree with this view but will not use this book to make the case, as others have done a sufficient job[8] I will just ask this: How do we expect to grow up into the fullness of who Christ is if we receive equipping from only two of the five people gifts? Is it any wonder the Church looks like a teaching center with care groups and has little (if any) missional, prophetic, and evangelistic ministry?

If you are wondering why there is so little evangelistic fruit, look around at your context. Do you see evangelists honored as gifts both setting an example to the believers in everyday life and training the body for evangelism formally and informally? Wonder why there is little to no multiplication of new groups, new ministries, and new churches? What have you done with the apostles? Have you sent them all overseas, left with no missionary impulse back home? It seemed very clear that many churches didn't know what to do the past couple of years as they rejected the prophets who were crying out against injustice and calling us back to faithfulness to God's Kingdom values. We need all five gifts serving (ministering) and equipping within the Church and in (and for) the world. Both activities are needed by all five of the people gifts. We need to see what each looks like and to be equipped by all five as well.

The word for *equip* in this text is the Greek word, *kartitizo*, which can be translated as *equip, perfect, mend, perfectly join together, put in order, ethically strengthen, complete, fulfill and heal*. If you put those words in Ephesians 4:11-12, it would read: "Jesus gave some to be apostles, prophets, evangelist, shepherds, and teachers to equip, perfect, mend, perfectly join together, put in order, ethically strengthen, complete, fulfill, and heal the saints for ministry (serving others like Jesus) so the whole body could be built up into a full and mature picture of Jesus in the world."

As we continue to apply this thinking to our context, remember to think beyond the church gathering to the Church scattered in everyday life. We are not equipping people only for our specific ministries. We are equipping them for the ministry (service) God has given them—which for most people is where they live, work, learn, and play.

The Fullness of Christ

The Church is not just the place you go to experience the fullness of Christ. The Church is the Body of Christ through which you are equipped to fulfill your calling in and to the world. Let's consider each people gift (A.P.E.S.T.), how it demonstrates Christ, and how it develops the Body toward the fullness of Christ.

Apostles

Apostles are pioneers who move outward to extend the Church's impact, developing the Church's identity as sent ones. They start and lay the foundation for new work. They tend to be less risk-averse and more innovative. Apostles catalyze and mobilize movement while easily adapting to new situations. As such, they serve as custodians of the gospel and the missional DNA of the Church.[9] We need apostles to continue to pioneer new works while they also equip every believer toward ongoing missional living.

Sondra Chamberlain was such an apostle, along with her husband Todd, who is a shepherd. When an opportunity opened at Lincoln High School to love and mentor varsity football players and the female locker room managers, Sondra mobilized her entire missional community to reinvest their energy into Lincoln's football program. The majority of the players didn't have a father present, so Sondra and Todd encouraged the men in the community to adopt players to be present with and support all year. The group provided a meal once a week after practice in the locker room, where a member would also share their testimony. Some of their homes became drop-in centers for the players to get a meal and some mentoring if needed. The players had an average GPA of 1.75 at the start of the year and 3.5 by the end. Many of the players also came to faith and were baptized in their high school's pool. When the school had to hire a new coach, the administration asked Sondra to be on the hiring committee. When they were looking to hire new faculty for the school, they recruited members from this community first. Sondra's life and example provided real opportunities for people to be equipped into their missionary identity.

Prophets

Prophets are hearers and seers who have vertical and horizontal functions. They harken back to what God has said and look forward to what God says will be. With eschatological ears and eyes, they call God's people to be a faithful expression of the Kingdom of God in a particular time and place. The vertical prophetic function exists to maintain our God-orientation. Prophets will do all they can to align their ears, eyes, mouth, and heart with God so they hear, see, speak, and feel what God does. The horizontal prophetic function exists to highlight our covenant relationship with God, worked out through how we live and love, calling people to repentance when needed. Prophets are agitators and agents of change. They serve to maintain the holy "soul" of the Church by speaking truth to power, being sensitive to spiritual warfare, distinguishing true and false worship, championing justice, calling us to holiness, and communicating urgency from a holy discontent.[10]

Brian Martin is a prophet. Brian and his wife, Alison, participated in foster care and eventually adopted. The more they and a few other prophets in our church observed the brokenness and needs of the foster system, the more engaged they became in providing solutions. They knew not everyone is called to foster children, but they also knew that God's Word is crystal clear about the Church's call to care for the lonely and orphans among us. Over the years they rallied our church to give significant time and resources to foster families. And because Alison is an evangelist, they especially wanted to care for families who were not yet connected to a church. There are now many missional communities that exist to serve foster families, looking to both show the love of Jesus in tangible form and to share it when given the opportunity. The Martins have equipped our church as a prophet-and-evangelist team, and the church looks more like Jesus the prophet and evangelist as a result.

Evangelists

Evangelists share the good news message of Jesus in embodied form with culturally expressed communication. They are exceptional recruiters to Jesus, the Kingdom, and the Kingdom cause and movement. They are persuasive and infectious people with appealing personalities. They really are *good news* people. Evangelists are consummate salespeople and marketers. They communicate in clear, compelling, and accessible ways, calling for a response in which they typically close "the deal." They tend to be winsome optimists who draw many in. Evangelists also create inviting, hospitable culture where many are attracted and all are welcomed. They regularly remind the Church that there are people to reach who are not yet here. We need evangelists to keep the Church facing outward and to train everyone to embody and share the good news.[11]

Kirby Apel is an evangelist. She was part of our missional community for many years. She is a joy to be around, and any space she shapes becomes warm, welcoming, and safe. She is also incredibly winsome! I remember telling Kirby that she was an evangelist, and she pushed back. I then reminded her how she convinced me to get up at Zero-Dark-Thirty in the morning for CrossFit three times a week and how she sold my wife on essential oils, then on Lip Sense. She even convinced my wife to join an indoor soccer team even though she had never played soccer and kind of despises running. Kirby can win you over to almost anything if she believes in it herself. She is an evangelist for anything she loves. No, she isn't on a stage, but life is her stage, and she is a very contagious person. Our missional community grew because of the attractive life she gave it.

Shepherds

Shepherds ensure that people are connected to community and are truly known and loved. They care for the hearts of people, protect them from harm, and work to bring about healing of wounds brought about by sin and evil. Shepherds are concerned with creating and maintaining healthy community, facilitating spiritual formation, promoting wholeness and reconciliation, encouraging people in the faith, and ensuring the welfare of the people as well as the broader society in which the Church abides. Shepherds have strong empathic aptitudes and heightened capacities for meaningful friendship and relationships. There are typically more shepherds in churches than any of the other five people gifts. I don't know whether that is because churches have historically been led by shepherds and thus attract like kind, or whether there are just more shepherds in the population because God knows we need many.[12]

Abe Meysenburg is a consummate shepherd. The team who first started Soma in Tacoma back in 2003 were largely apostles, prophets, and evangelists, which is actually a good mix for starting a new work. However, we certainly lacked in the area of shepherd equipping until Abe showed up. He had also started a new church, but it was lacking in what we had. So we merged our two churches, and Abe the shepherd came with a teaching gift. Abe was a great example of a shepherd who deeply cared for the flock. He also built a strong equipping pathway to raise up skilled shepherds and to ensure that our disciple-making environments were safe, caring spaces.

Jayne, my wife, is also a shepherd. She happens to be a prophet as well. These two gifts have led her to be an EMT (emergency medical technician) who transports people in critical conditions to places where they can get the care they need. She had volunteered for Hospice Care for 15 years prior to being trained to be an EMT. She absolutely loves being with people in their worst situations and provides an amazing amount of care by bringing calm to people in trauma.

Teachers

Lastly, teachers. Teachers are committed to mediating a particular type of practical wisdom and philosophical understanding nuanced by the biblical worldview. They can make wisdom and insight accessible and applicable. Teachers will largely be concerned with helping people gain insight into how God wants them to see and experience their world. They are committed to cultivating a love of Scripture and engaging in theological discourse. They are committed to the broad comprehension and systematic understanding of key ideas and philosophies that shape all of life. They are not content with ideas or philosophies alone. They want to help people integrate them into everyday life and thinking. Skilled teachers are great at creating learning environments that are geared more toward practical application.[13]

A person that comes to my mind as I write this is Ben Connelly. I believe Ben may be an apostle first, as he has shown himself to be proficient at starting new things. But a close second is his gift of being a teacher. Ben is brilliant at creating learning environments for all kinds of learners. He can take big ideas and make them accessible. He doesn't just talk; he facilitates genuine learning that leads to practice. Ben has developed curriculum for Bible studies, book studies (including co-writing workbooks for two of my books), disciple-making, church planting, and more. But his best contribution, in my opinion, are the environments he facilitates for learning. Ben now leads a ministry called The Equipping Group, where he leverages not only his gift but the gifts of many others for equipping the church.

Apostles equip the saints as sent ones. Prophets equip us to bring a holy presence. Evangelists equip us to share the good news. Shepherds equip us for soul care. Teachers equip us to learn and apply God's truth. We need all five.

Consider your context. Do the people in your church or ministry have access to all five (A.P.E.S.T.) types of people on a regular basis? Can they observe their lives and ministry? And do they have opportunities to be equipped by them as well? Or has your church taken the captives who Jesus set free and put them back into captivity in service to a few ministers who have also returned to a form of captivity themselves as they try to do it all on their own?

As opposed to being immature disciples, Paul challenges us by saying, "But speaking the truth in love, let us grow in every way into him who is the head–Christ. From him the whole body, fitted and knit together by every supporting ligament, promotes the growth of the body for building itself up in love by the proper working of each individual part" (Ephesians 4:15-16, CSB).

We need all five kinds of gifted people to equip, speak, and lead by example. We need everyone set free and equipped to practice living out the gift they are to the Church. As every part works properly, every part equips the others. We aren't just called to equip the ministers. Every believer is called to grow up into an equipper as well.

Every believer, a minister. Every minister, an equipper.

Everyone free to serve and be served.

All for the purpose of expressing Jesus more fully and making him known both to those currently in the family of God and those not yet a part.

So, how do we create effective equipping opportunities for all five?

NOTES

1. John 20:21; Hebrews 3:1, 12:2

2. Mark 1:15; Luke 4:14-20; Matthew 5:7

3. Luke 4:18, 43; 7:22; 16:16

4. John 10:11, 14-16; 1 Peter 2:25

5. John 14:6, 9

6. Colossians 2:2-3

7. One of these voices was John Calvin. I deeply appreciate many of Calvin's works. However, I do believe he was wrong in concluding that the only gifts needed are Shepherd and Teacher. I wonder whether his being in Geneva, which at the time of Calvin, was largely Christian, influenced his conclusions since it didn't appear to need Evangelists or Apostles, though one could argue it certainly needed Prophets.

8. Some resources for further study are: *The Permanent Revolution: Apostolic Imagination and Practice for the 21st Century Church* by Alan Hirsch and Tim Catchim; *The Forgotten Ways: Reactivating Apostolic Movements* by Alan Hirsch; Fathering Leaders, Motivating Mission: Restoring the Role of the Apostle in Today's Church by David Devenish.

9. Some examples of the types of people who fit the description of Apostle are movement leaders, church planters, innovators, pioneers, entrepreneurs, organization architects and designers, cross-cultural missionaries, networkers, designers and architects, consultants, and ambassadors.

10. Some examples of the types of people who fit the description of Prophet are intercessors; social activists and campaigners; holy dissenters; questioners of the status quo; prayer and deliverance ministers; artists, poets, and musicians; protestors; aid and development workers; investigators; mystics and deep thinkers; and whistle-blowers.

11. Some examples of the types of people who fit the description of Evangelist are crusade workers or speakers, recruiters, salespeople, entrepreneurs, apologists, communications and media workers, marketers, storytellers, producers and directors, journalists, and networkers.

12. Some examples of the types of people who fit the description of Shepherd are pastoral care-givers, spiritual directors, counselors, doctors/nurses/therapists, community developers, relational networkers, recreational workers, human resource workers, social workers, police and defense personnel, and guardians or defenders.

13. Some examples of the types of people who fit the description of Teacher are instructors/trainers, mentors/coaches, educators, theologians, philosophers, writers, thinkers, truth-tellers, researchers, guides, and wise sages.

* What is one thing you yearn for when you get a break/ off work?

* What does yar ♥ desire....

*

CHAPTER FIVE

The Equipping Process

I've seen it happen over and over again. Leaders recognize that they aren't equipping people to become disciple-making disciples. They know they need to make some changes. Sometimes they bring in outside counsel, but in far too many cases they merely add classes, curriculum, and teaching. Some do better and create new environments like small groups or missional communities. However, most of them make the same mistake. They think if they just give people new information and new teaching, they will become equipped. But new information alone is not enough to equip God's people for ministry.

I know, I know, I'm writing a book full of information making a statement that information alone doesn't equip. To be honest, that is why I've been hesitant to write books over the years. I know books alone are not sufficient to equip people. As a speaker, I also know speaking is not sufficient. Books and speeches can inform, inspire, and bring conviction where it may have been lacking. They can spur on imagination and creativity as well as motivate toward action. Information is part of equipping, but it is the least-effective form if informing is all we do. People don't learn new skills and behaviors just by being told. They need a more holistic approach to equipping. They need D.E.E.P.E.R. equipping.

D.E.E.P.E.R. Equipping

I was mentored by leaders who encouraged me to keep studying the life and ministry of Jesus to discern and develop strategies for making disciples. As an intuitive leader looking at Jesus' strategy, I was able to build a more holistic approach to equipping. Over the years, a pattern emerged. Regardless of whether I was working with teenagers or a core group for a new church plant, there was a consistent pattern—what I now call D.E.E.P.E.R. training.[1] D.E.E.P.E.R. stands for Demonstrate, Experience, Explain, Practice, Expose, Reflect—then Repeat until you can Reproduce (yes, that's three Rs at the end). The most effective equipping I've been involved in embodied D.E.E.P.E.R. training. The least effective was merely lecturing.

Demonstrate

D—Demonstrate it so they can see it.

When learning a new thing, you must see it to get it. I am still learning to golf. One of the greatest equipping practices for me is watching a good golf swing. I must see it over and over again to recognize what it looks like and where my swing is still lacking. So to equip others effectively, we demonstrate first.

Jesus came to earth, taking on human flesh, to demonstrate how to live so we can see what true living looks like. Jesus demonstrated for his disciples everything he trained them to do. They saw him heal the sick, give sight to the blind, cast out demons, proclaim good news, show compassion, and eat with outsiders. They watched Jesus protect the vulnerable and care for the weak. They saw Jesus pray. They observed Jesus confront the religious leaders and then submit himself to their collusion with the Roman occupation to have him crucified. Some of his followers witnessed him praying from the cross for those who persecuted him. At one point, Philip asked Jesus to show them the Father. Jesus' response was, "Anyone who has seen me has seen the Father" (John 14:9). Jesus demonstrated the loving heart of the Father in everything he did.

Think about all the things you would love to see people trained in. Think about your context. Have you provided ways for them to see what you are training them to do? One way we can do this is through story. Stories can create mental imagery for equipping. When I am training a larger group of people who don't have access to my everyday life, the best I can do is tell stories. Biblical stories about Jesus create mental pictures for us as well. However, the ideal is always a real person doing it in front of us and doing it often.

Some of my best disciple-making training has been done on the mission field of everyday life. I would regularly bring guys I was training along with me into my everyday mission. One of my favorite memories was taking a young man to a lunch spot I frequented, where I had become quite familiar with several of the servers. One particular woman often waited on my table. During our lunch I asked her how she was doing. She started to tear up and said, "I know when you ask you actually want the truth because you care." For her to see that required consistency from me. I had eaten at that same restaurant many times before she concluded this about me. She went on to share with us that she had moved to Tacoma and purchased a fixer-upper house. She worked all day at the restaurant and worked every night on the house. But she was in over her head. She continued describing how the house now had torn-out walls and ripped-up floors, and she didn't know what to do. She was overwhelmed and felt all alone. The guy with me that day happened to be a carpenter. He and I agreed immediately that we would help her. She couldn't believe it! Over the coming months several of us helped her remodel her home. One Sunday morning I looked out at our young congregation and saw her in the back. That day she gave her life to Jesus and shared how our love for her in action convinced her that Jesus loved her as well. That young man saw me demonstrate how to care for others. He also experienced it himself.

Experience

D—Demonstrate it so they can see it.

E—Experience it so they can feel it.

People need to experience something to know what it feels like. The best way for this to happen is by either doing what you are training *to* them or at least *with* them. Back to my golf swing. I've had people help me swing a club correctly so I can feel what a good swing feels like. So much of Jesus' equipping was done through him doing something *to* another or doing something *with* or *through* another. After a day of catching no fish, Jesus called the disciples to cast their net on the other side of the boat, and they experienced a miraculous catch. Later, Jesus miraculously fed the 5,000 through the hands of his disciples. Jesus also called Peter to walk on the water to him, and when he sank, Peter felt Jesus pulling him up. The disciples experienced Jesus teaching them about the Kingdom of God. They also experienced Jesus correcting and even rebuking them when they were wrong or out of line. They experienced table fellowship with Jesus alone, and they also experienced eating with sinners and tax collectors.

Again, consider your own context. Are people merely hearing you talk about the things you want them to be equipped in, or are they experiencing them personally? Are you creating training opportunities that they can see *and* feel?

I wanted to train the guys I was equipping in listening prayer. I invited a small group of them to join me two or three mornings a week. I asked them to bring their Bible, a journal, and a writing utensil. Each time, we would ask the Spirit to speak, read some Scripture, sit in silence, and then begin to write what we sensed the Spirit was saying to us. After some time, I invited each one to share what he heard. I wanted them to experience listening, not just be told about it. Then, I explained how we can discern whether or not something is from God's Spirit. (It must agree with Scripture; we submit it to one another; and whatever we hear should sound like what Jesus would say or lead us to do.)

Explain

> **D**—Demonstrate it so they can see it.
>
> **E**—Experience it so they can feel it.
>
> **E**—Explain it so they can hear it.

Even though explaining or communicating something is not in itself sufficient to fully equip someone, you also can't faithfully equip someone without explaining the truth. We need to speak the truth so they hear it.

I know the concepts of what makes up a good golf swing because I read books and blogs about it, and I listen to experts talk about it. Jesus often pulled his disciples aside and explained what he was doing and why he was doing it. If they didn't understand a parable, he explained it to them. When they didn't know how to cast out a demon, he explained what was necessary. When they asked Jesus how to pray, he told them to pray like this, "Our Father in heaven, hallowed be your name. Your kingdom come, your will be done, on earth as it is in heaven. Give us today our daily bread. And forgive us our debts, as we also have forgiven our debtors. And lead us not into temptation but deliver us from the evil one."[2] When they refused to allow little children to come near to Jesus, he said, "Let the little children come to me, and do not hinder them, for the kingdom of heaven belongs to such as these."[3] We absolutely need to declare the truth. We must share the truth to equip people well. We can't have transformation without declaring truthful information.

This is probably the area you are already strong in. However, consider how often your equipping comes from sources other than God's Word. Yes, "wisdom cries out in the street,"[4] and we are wise to listen to and heed and teach all forms of wisdom and truth. Yet we also need to make sure the ultimate source of our equipping is based upon biblical truth. And even more crucial, our equipping must line up with and conform to the gospel of Jesus Christ.

I remember one morning prayer session listening to one of the young men in the group praying. He never referred to God as "Father," and his prayers sounded like he believed he had to convince God to care about him. He had come from a very abusive home where his father physically and verbally abused him and then abandoned the family. So it was entirely understandable for him to struggle with seeing God as a good, loving Father. With that said, we still needed to explain to him that Jesus reveals a very different picture of the Father than his dad did. We described the love of the Father and asked the Spirit to make the Father's heart known to him. During that time, we watched the Spirit pour the love of the Father into his heart,[5] and it transformed his prayer life. We explained the Father's love, and he experienced the Father's love.

Practice

D—Demonstrate so they can see it.

E—Experience so they can feel it.

E—Explain so they can hear it.

P—Practice so they can do it.

No one learns something well by doing it once. We become equipped in a new practice or behavior by doing it over and over again. This is common sense.

Golf instructor Hank Haney recommended a minimum of 100 golf swings a day to become a good golfer. There's a reason I'm still not that good. I don't practice enough. Jesus spent more than three years with his disciples. He called them to put into practice his teaching. At one point, he told the story of a wise man who built his house on a rock versus the fool who built his house on the sand. His intention was to demonstrate the difference between someone who hears Jesus' words (explain) and does them (practice) and the one who merely hears but does not put them into practice.[6] When Jesus sent his disciples out in pairs, he was sending them out to practice what he had been training them to do. When I think about how often we give people information with little to no expectation that they go practice it, then we give them new additional information that they will not put into practice, it makes me shudder! What are we doing?! We are leading people to practice foolishness. Why give more teaching when people are not practicing what you have already taught?

Are you calling people to put into practice what you are teaching? What kinds of practice are you giving them? How do you know if they are getting better?

In 2015 I was asked to step into what remained of Mars Hill Bellevue and start a new church. Mars Hill Sammamish joined us as well. We called the new church Doxa Church. I took everything I had learned and previously trained our Soma churches to do and tried to repeat it with Doxa. Several years in we learned that many of our people had the information and even some training, but they lacked the motivation and empowerment that comes from abiding in Christ. We had assumed they were well developed in spiritual practices like solitude, silence, sabbath, prayer, Bible reading, and such. It turned out many knew about these practices but had not been equipped well in them. In response, we decided to pick one spiritual practice a quarter. We used the D.E.E.P.E.R. template to equip them. We created several ways for them to practice incrementally. For example, with silence, we started by giving a teaching (explanation) in our gathering that we also captured on video for people to go back and watch or listen to. Then we created a short space in our weekly gatherings to practice silence. As a first step, we invited people to turn their music or podcast off while on their commute. Then, we suggested they try setting aside a weekly space and time for 10-20 minutes of silence. Eventually, we led them to practice silence and solitude in one-hour, then two-hour, then half-a-day increments. We decided to only do one new spiritual practice every three months to create the space for practice. We did one practice a quarter for three years.[7] Over time, people were more effectively equipped in the spiritual practices as a result.

Expose

D—Demonstrate so they can see it.

E—Experience so they can feel it.

E—Explain so they can hear it.

P—Practice so they can do it.

E—Expose so what's inside is revealed.

In equipping someone, we want the true, authentic person to show up. Real development happens when the truth comes out.

Back to my golf game. Just one round of golf will expose the cracks in my game—and in my emotional stability! Take people on a mission trip, and you will discover what they are really like. Put them together in a missional community and call them to love one another and serve those God puts in their pathway, and you find out what's really inside.

Jesus sent his disciples out, and their hearts were revealed when they came back. Some of them took a long walk, and before long they were arguing over who is the greatest. Jesus invited them to join him in prayer during his most trying hour in the Garden of Gethsemane, and they fell asleep. When the guards came, a knife cut off an ear. After Jesus died, they went back to fishing. And even after Jesus had risen, they still doubted. Not their finest moments, but authentic just the same. This step in equipping is not meant to shame people. Exposure is about bringing to light what was in the dark so that it can be addressed and transformed.

As a soccer coach, I had my players do drills with both feet so that I could expose their weak side. Then we would work to strengthen that foot—not to embarrass them or make them self-conscious, but so the opposing team wouldn't take advantage. We did weak-foot drills over and over again to improve their confidence and develop their skills.

Our equipping needs to bring exposure so we can become aware of what still needs to be developed and so the enemy doesn't take advantage. We want to expose doubt, fear, ignorance, lack of skill, character defects, and more. If we are going to holistically equip people, we must see the whole person.

Does your equipping methodology create opportunities for exposure? Does your environment make it safe to fail? Do you lead by example in revealing your weaknesses and areas for growth? A development culture is a place where it is normal to be needy, where weakness is welcomed, and where failure is familiar. Equipping environments make it normative for the real person to show up so we equip people from where they truly are.

I remember stepping in to coach one of our very broken missional communities. They had a wonderful opportunity to love and share Jesus with the boating culture. Every weekend these friends joined several other boaters on the water for wakeboarding, surfing, feasting, and fun. (There were a lot of really inappropriate activities going on as well.) As I got more involved and became more acquainted with what was happening, I realized that we needed to back up and provide some better training. We put a pause on the missional activities and worked instead on character development and gospel-centered, missional living.

I remember one of the first events we engaged in after some training. A couple of people in our group decided to host a Super Bowl party. After the party we debriefed about how it went. Half of the group thought it went really well. The other half said it was terrible. I asked why. The first group said they thought it was great because they spent most of the time showing the non-Christians how wrong they were. The second group said, "That's why it was so bad!" Exposure happened. Now we could address the issue. I didn't shame them, but we took the time to reconsider what hospitality and kindness looks like. Later that year, that same group went away for an extended weekend on a lake with some of the same friends. This time they created a space for each person who wanted to share their story. The Christians shared their stories, with Jesus as the hero. The non-Christians felt safe to share their stories as well. It was an entirely different experience.

Reflect

D—Demonstrate so they can see it.

E—Experience so they can feel it.

E—Explain so they can hear it.

P—Practice so they can do it.

E—Expose so what's inside is revealed.

R—Reflect so they can process.

Stepping back and considering what we've done or how we've applied what we've learned is crucial. We need feedback. We need to process. Too often we "train" people in a skill and never create space to process their experience and practice. Exposure needs to be followed by reflection.

One of the best ways for me to improve my golf swing is by watching a video of my swing with someone who can help me process what I did right or wrong and then agree on what needs to change. Again, Jesus did this with his disciples regularly. The clearest example is after they returned from their paired-up mission trip.

During this part of our equipping, we ask a lot of questions: What was that like for you? What did you experience? How did it go? What did you discover? What would you do differently next time? What do you now know you need? How can we help you prepare?

That is what we did with the boater missional community. It's also what we did when we were training people to teach in a gathering. Not only did we follow the D.E.E.P.E.R. template, but we created space after delivering a message in front of a small group for reflection and feedback. We provided additional feedback between the first and second gathering on a Sunday, and then even more feedback after. Those who were in the equipping process, but not yet up to teach, also observed this so they too could be equipped through demonstration, experience, explanation, practice, exposure, and reflection.

After reflection, we lead people to repeat the process until they are proficient enough to reproduce what they've been trained to do. And our hope is that our equipping is both D.E.E.P.E.R. and diverse, representing the fullness of Christ by involving apostles, prophets, evangelists, shepherds, and teachers. That is how we develop an equipping process that multiplies disciple-making disciples who are being equipped into the fullness of Christ.

NOTES

1. For more on D.E.E.P.E.R. Training go to saturatetheworld.com and search for D.E.E.P.E.R. Training.
2. Mathew 6:9-13
3. Matthew 19:14
4. Proverbs 1:20-21
5. Romans 5:5
6. Matthew 7:24-27
7. You can look at the Doxa Church app if you're interested in learning more about how we did this. I'd also recommend John Mark Comer's "Practicing the Way" resources.

CHAPTER SIX

Designing an Equipping Strategy

Start with an Assessment

Think about your present context. Are you equipping people in the fullness of Christ and in holistic ways that are much more than just informing?

We are helping people identify the kind of people gift they are.

1   2   3   4   5   6   7   8   9   10

Our equipping is diverse (A.P.E.S.T.).

1   2   3   4   5   6   7   8   9   10

Our equipping is holistic (D.E.E.P.E.R.).

1   2   3   4   5   6   7   8   9   10

All people are affirmed as ministers.

1   2   3   4   5   6   7   8   9   10

Every aspect of life is affirmed as ministry

1   2   3   4   5   6   7   8   9   10

Which people gift is missing in our equipping or needs more attention?

Which skills are we presently equipping people in?

Of these, which ones embody DEEPER?

What part of our equipping is lacking a holistic approach, and what is missing?

What needs to change, and what needs the most attention?

Equipping Buildout

Considering your definition of a disciple and your disciple-making pathway, with which skills or practices do you need to equip disciples?

Choose one of the skills to build out an equipping template that is D.E.E.P.E.R.

(Repeat this process with every skill)

How will you **Demonstrate** it (so they see it)?

How will they **Experience** it (so they feel it)?

How will we **Explain** it, and what will we explain (so they hear it)?

How will we lead them to **Practice** it (so they do it)?

How will we help them to be **Exposed** (so what is inside is revealed)? What questions will we ask?

How will we help them to **Reflect** on it (so they process it)? What questions will we ask?

FROM ATTENDING TO ATTACHING

FROM ATTENDING TO ATTACHING

Paul told Timothy (1 Timothy 1:5) that the purpose of his instruction is love from a pure heart and a sincere faith, reflecting Jesus' words that the greatest commandment is to love God with all we are and to love our neighbor as we love ourselves. Jesus takes it even further and says that we are also to love our enemies.

Love, according to the Bible, is giving of yourself to another. Jesus said, "For God so loved the world that he gave his one and only son" (John 3:16). This love is not merely a feeling but a true giving of one's whole self in a genuine relationship. More recently, people are calling this "attachment love." This is not new. God has always existed in a self-giving form of love in the Trinity, and he invites us into a relationship where we can also attach to his self-giving love.

The role of leadership in the church is not just to create programs for people to attend but to create relational spaces to help people lovingly attach to God and others. That is the third shift we need to make—a shift from attending to attaching. Far too many churches and ministries have slipped into merely running programs for people to attend, forgetting the purposes for which the programs exist. Jesus didn't say that we would know who his disciples were by their attendance. Jesus said his disciples would be known by their love for one another, so we need to ask whether our programs are creating space for people to grow in loving attachment to God and others.

Let's first look at the dynamic of social spaces and how they contribute to developing loving attachment in our relationships. Then we will consider how we engage in spiritual practices with the goal of growing in attachment love in each of the social spaces.

CHAPTER SEVEN

Creating Disciple-Making Spaces

Alex Absalom and Bobby Harrington, drawing from Joseph R. Myer's work, *The Search to Belong*, which drew from the pioneering 1960s sociologist Edward T. Hall's theory of proxemics, wrote a very helpful book called *Discipleship That Fits*. In the book, they unpack the dynamics of social space and intentional disciple-making. (I highly recommend their book if you want to take a deeper look at the concepts of this chapter.) For our purposes, I want you to consider whether your present ministry is thinking strategically about creating and engaging different relational spaces for the sake of making mature disciples of Jesus who are growing in attachment love.

Let's examine each of the five key relational spaces: divine, transparent, personal, social, and public.

Divine Space

Jesus often withdrew to solitary places to be alone with the Father. Jesus was truly attached in loving relationship with his Father, and he consistently cultivated this relational space. Consider his words in John 5:19, "Very truly I tell you, the Son can do nothing by himself; he can only do what he sees his Father doing. Because whatever the Father does the Son also does." In response to Philip saying, "Show us the Father," Jesus asks in John 14:9-11: "Don't you know me, Philip, even after I have been among you such a long time? Anyone who has seen me has seen the Father. How can you say, 'Show us the Father'? Don't you believe that I am in the Father, and that the Father is in me? The words I say to you I do not speak on my own authority. Rather, it is the Father, living in me, who is doing his work. Believe me when I say that I am in the Father and the Father is in me; or at least believe on the evidence of the works themselves."

Jesus then calls his disciples and all who will believe him to the same kind of relationship with him and with God the Father through the Spirit in John 14. He promises that he will not leave us alone like orphans but will send the Spirit to be with us, teach us, and empower us to do the same works that he did. Jesus further clarifies in John 15 that we must abide in him and he in us if we are going to bear fruit. Apart from him we can do nothing (just like Jesus could do nothing apart from the Father). Jesus goes on to declare that the fruit we will bear is expressed in loving one another. Later, in John 17:21 we hear Jesus pray "that all of them may be one, Father, just as you are in me and I am in you. May they also be in us so that the world may believe that you have sent me."

It is out of this divine space of intimate attachment to the love of God the Father, God the Son, and God the Holy Spirit that everything else flows. In fact, Jesus is very clear that those who love (lovingly attach to) him will obey him. We don't obey to prove our love to Jesus. We obey as an outcome of our love from and for Jesus. We are in him and he is in us. It is attachment love that compels us to obey him.

We have wrongly believed for far too long that we are changed by just thinking new thoughts. Michel Hendricks, in the book he co-authored with Jim Wilder, *The Other Half of Church*,[1] states it this way, "Many Western Christians believe character is formed by thinking correctly, believing truth, and making wise choices in light of the truth. If all of this is empowered by the Holy Spirit, we are on the path to Christian maturity. This is the philosophy I used to help people grow in their faith," he recalls. He even remembers saying during one training that "to change our character, we need to change our thinking." The problem with this conclusion, according to the book's authors, is that it is "half-brained." It assumes that we are primarily formed through left-brained development (language, logical thinking, problem solving, and strategies).

However, our beliefs and doctrine (formulated in the left brain) are created from knowing the relational love of God (formulated in the right brain). In other words, you do not come to know and believe in God, who is love, without first relationally and emotionally experiencing the love of God. This is why 1 John 4 says that we love God because God first loved us. John continues by saying that if we know (relational engagement) and abide (attachment) in God (who is love), we will abide in love and will love others as a result. This is all right-brained activity that cannot be formed simply by engaging in left-brained processes.[2]

My friends started a wonderful new ministry called Eden Project. They want to help people learn to be at home once again in the love of the Father. They acknowledge that most of our present formation strategies are left-brain dominant, and as a result people are theologically informed but emotionally and spiritually deformed. They know a lot about God but don't know how to lovingly attach to him. Nathan Wagnon (author and CEO of Eden Project) did his dissertation on our "God image" in relation to our "God concept." He concludes that most of us have a God image (how we actually experience, view, and relate to God) that doesn't line up with our God concept (what we say we believe is true about God). For instance, many of us would say we believe God is love (left-brained doctrine/truth); however, when we pray or sabbath or engage in silence and solitude, we find ourselves relating to a very different version of God (right-brained/relating). This image of God for many of us is demanding or demeaning, looking down on us in condemnation, not with loving affection and acceptance. The reason our image does not line up with our concept is because we are formed more by our *relations* (right-brained) than our *ideas* (left-brained). How our parents lovingly attached or reservedly detached shaped our view of God significantly. The people we experience life with at work, at home, and in church continue to form our view of God significantly. The way back to the kind of relationship God intended is not just through our thinking, though this is necessary. The way back is through a renewed view of God through relationships that are healing and restorative. We don't just need new concepts or ideas about God. We need new relational experiences with God and others that transform our relational image of God as well.

This reality has led many to seek out spiritual directors like my friend Chuck Gschwend (part of Eden Project), who helps people reconnect to the love of God the Father relationally. As you think about your present context and the relational spaces you create for making disciples, seriously consider how you help people learn to relationally attach to our God, who is love, as they relationally attach to one another as well.

Transparent Space

We can discern how well people are lovingly attaching to God by how they love others. And people love others based upon the love and care they have for themselves. Your external life is always the outflow of your internal life, which is why Jesus says it is not what goes into a person that corrupts but what comes out of a person.[3] He also said it is out of the overflow of the heart that the mouth speaks.[4] Jesus said we are to love others as we love ourselves.[5]

There is an appropriate kind of self-love that is often missing in our formational work. We misunderstand passages where Jesus tells us to deny ourselves and take up our cross as some kind of call to self-hatred. However, we must remember, we are made in the image of God. As Psalm 139:13-14 states, we are "fearfully and wonderfully made," and we are called to praise God's work—which includes us! Ephesians 2:10 tells us that we are "[God's] workmanship, created in Christ Jesus for good works that he prepared in advance for us to do." The word *workmanship* comes from the Greek word *poiema*, from where we also get the word *poem*. We are a work of art created by God. If we hate ourselves, we are hating God's workmanship. Loving God includes loving ourselves as part of his workmanship. And loving others is only possible when we love God and who God made us to be. You can only love others to the degree in which you have received love yourself.

This is why we need transparent space. We need a place where two or other people can see the truth about us. This is where we get back to Genesis 2 and learn to be figuratively "naked and unashamed"[6] with a few others. If we're married, ideally this is primarily our spouse, although sadly, people in many marriages are living hidden lives from one another. The way back to true intimacy with a spouse may start with a few other trusted people we can be transparent with so that we can get the courage to bring our full self to our spouse again.

Transparent space is where a few others know our full story, understand our struggles, and see how we do or do not care for our body, mind, and soul. These people journey with us through the highs and lows of life and remind us of how loved we are and what is true for us in Christ. Sometimes, what we need most in this space is what Job needed from his friends—a non-anxious presence that doesn't try to fix us.

Jesus had a few close friends whom he became transparent with. He had Peter, James, and John in his inner circle. It was to these three men that Jesus revealed himself most fully through his transfiguration.[7] Jesus also took Peter, James, and John with him as he agonized over facing the cross while praying in the Garden of Gethsemane.[8] His friends sadly failed him, but after his resurrection he went back to them so they could reaffirm their love and restore their relationship.

Transparent space is a safe place for us to fully show up. With most of our Soma Churches, we call this space a DNA (Discuss/Nurture/Act) group or a triad. Some churches call these spaces LTGs (Life Transformation Groups). It is in these safe places where we can talk about what we know and believe to be true; share honestly about our fear, hurt, sadness, and doubts; and lovingly lead one another to submit to Jesus for the help, healing, and comfort we need. It is in this space where our truest image of God and self are revealed, if given the attention and direction. Unfortunately, far too many of these spaces use fear, shame, and guilt to motivate behavior change, leading people to hide through deception or performance. This doesn't lead to heart-level transformation. It merely creates manipulated behavior modification.

Do you have space like this in your present context?[9] How are you stewarding it to allow for people to truly show up with transparency and vulnerability?

Personal Space

Personal space consists of our close circle of friends who we feel comfortable sharing personal information with. Our love for one another gets expressed, practiced, and tested in personal space. We have enough access to one another to encourage and build one another up, as well as correct and confront when necessary. We experience a genuine depth of relationship in this space. Most of us can do this with 10-20 people. It is in this space where we practice the "one anothers." It is also here that we discover where we still need to grow in love. Ideally, those with whom we share transparent space are engaged or at least have access to how we respond to others in our personal space. When that is the case, personal space provides the environment for those closest to us to see how we're growing in love through our divine and transparent spaces.

Jesus had personal space with his twelve disciples and the women disciples (at least five we know by name) who were very close to him during his ministry. They ate meals together, learned together, traveled together, and served others together. They watched Jesus' life and ministry as well as his death and resurrection. They did life together in community through the good, the bad, and the ugly. Some expressions of this space with Jesus are the time in the boat during the storm, processing Jesus' teaching together, Jesus washing his disciples' feet, and sharing the Passover meal.

Most churches have this space in place. They are often called small groups or life groups. Unfortunately, many of these groups don't "do" much life together outside of a few hours together in a formal meeting. And many are limited to merely doing a Bible study together at best. Bible study is good, but if we never experience life together in community outside a formal study, it's likely that people don't really know one another very well, and very little relational transformation takes place.

Do you have personal space for people to grow in love for one another? Are there relationships growing in genuine depth of love that extend beyond a weekly meeting so that people are practicing the "one anothers"?

Social Space

In our social space we share snapshots of who we are, and we seek to build affinity with others. Myers points out that in this context (think of a backyard grill out) three things happen: we build neighborly relations (people we can call upon for minor favors), we start to identify those with whom we'd like to become closer friends, and we reveal elements of our identity and our journey. This space is generally shared with 20-70 people.

It is in this space that we learn to practice hospitality, making space for people to feel at home with us just as they are. This is where the sojourner and the stranger can find community. Outsiders have the opportunity to become friends in this space. It is also through this space where a larger group of people can collectively serve others, making a significant impact on a particular people and place.

Jesus engaged this space. We witness Jesus and his disciples at the wedding feast in Cana, where he makes the party better by bringing the better wine. Jesus and his disciples join Matthew the tax collector and friends for a party, and Jesus also goes to Zacchaeus' house to celebrate. Shortly after his transfiguration, we see Jesus appoint the 70 disciples.

Many churches do not intentionally create or engage in social space. Churches with missional communities or their equivalent engage this space more effectively. Most of our Soma churches help their missional communities identify a group of people who are not yet connected to Jesus and his family, the Church, to serve and celebrate together, with the goal of seeing them move from outsiders to friends to family.

Is this type of space intentionally designed or engaged in your context?[10] How effective are the people you lead at loving the outsider and stranger?

Public Space

In public space, we have a shared experience and are often inspired or moved in a particular way, but we don't generally know everyone, nor do we expect to get too personal or close to anyone. This space usually includes more than 70 people and upward to hundreds or thousands. The focus in this space is on engaging with something outside us, rather than building relational depth with others who also happen to be there. This can be a public event like a concert, a sporting event, or a recreational activity. For the Church, this is often our weekly gathering.

Jesus certainly engaged this space but didn't expect much from it. He spoke to the crowds and fed them, when necessary, but he also saw that his time with the crowds had little lasting impact. It allowed him to declare who he is and what he is committed to do, but he didn't make disciples of the crowd. Some were called out of the crowd to follow him, but public space by nature does not allow for relational attachment and transformation. In fact, in John 6 we see the crowds leave Jesus once he called them to look to him for true sustenance. Later, Jesus weeps over Jerusalem because its people were like lost sheep without a shepherd.

People are drawn to this shared public space. People want to be with others who have similar interests or pursuits. As the Church gathers in public space, we do have an opportunity to form people through shared experience where the good news is proclaimed. We need to engage this space well but also not expect more from this space than is possible. I find that this is one of the areas we need to speak more realistically about. I believe most churches put the majority of their energy and resources into this space, believing it can do more than it actually does. Sadly, we are deceived by attendance numbers into believing that if the crowd grows, we are accomplishing Jesus' mission. But remember, his mission isn't attendance. His mission is helping people attach to the love of the Father, Son, and Holy Spirit, leading them to love others and themselves with the love they are actively experiencing with God. This is at the heart of making disciples of Jesus.

How are you engaging this space? Has it received too much attention and resources or not enough?

We need to address all these spaces if we are going to make holistic disciples of Jesus who make disciples. Public gatherings are important, but they are not sufficient. We need to train disciples to not just attend these spaces but to learn how to lovingly attach to God and others through these spaces. To do that, we need to consider how the spiritual practices in each space can lead to true, transformative attachment love with God and others.

NOTES

1. *The Other Half of Church: Christian Community, Brain Science, and Overcoming Spiritual Stagnation* by Jim Wilder and Michel Hendricks is a very helpful resource to read as we consider how we design our activities to spur on attachment love in the Church. They lay out what right-brained development looks like in our spiritual and communal practices.

2. On page 28 of *The Other Half of Church*, the authors describe how the brain works: "The right brain integrates our life, including our connection to loved ones, our bodies, our surroundings, our emotions, our identities, and our community. Character formation flows out of these connections." The writers continue, "Our right brain depends on relational input to form our character." So, if we are going to develop disciples in love, we will have to do right-brain activity and development.

3. Matthew 15:11

4. Matthew 12:34

5. Matthew 23:39

6. The Hebrew word for *naked* in Genesis 2 is different from the word for *naked* in Genesis 3. In Genesis 2 the word means "unclothed," with nothing relationally keeping the man and the woman from being connected and receiving what they needed from God and one another. They felt no need to hide from each other. In Genesis 3, after they ate of the fruit of the tree of knowledge of good and evil, the nakedness they experienced was a shame over their need for one another that led to a relational poverty with God and one another. The response was a need to hide from God and one another.

7. Matthew 17:1-8

8. Matthew 26:36-46

9. Some organizations provide great resources for developing safe, transparent spaces and experiences. Some of these organizations are Eden Project, Tin Man Ministries, and Saturate.

10. If you want to learn from groups who do this well, look at Kansas City Underground, Tampa Underground, the Soma Family of Churches, and We Are Church. Saturatetheworld.com also has plenty of resources about how to start, lead, and strengthen missional communities.

CHAPTER EIGHT

Growing in Love Through Spiritual Practices

Jesus said that he came to give life and to give it to the full. He promised an abundant, flourishing life. And yet, he said this life is only possible for those who would follow him. To follow Jesus never meant to observe him from afar with wonder and amazement, like watching a great athlete or actor perform their craft. Jesus said, "If any of you wants to be my follower, you must give up your own way, take up your cross, and follow me."[1] Jesus invites us to walk in his way, and his way is the way of love, laying down his life out of love for us. Sadly, far too many want the abundant life without walking in the way of Jesus.

The spiritual practices are meant to lead us into the way. They are not an end in themselves but a means. They are meant to lead us to attachment love with God and others. Jesus said, "Now, this is eternal life [abundant life—life that is truly living]: that they know [attach with] you, the only true God, and Jesus Christ whom you have sent."[2] Jesus continues, praying that all who believe in him will be intimately connected to God the Father and God the Son through God the Spirit.[3] The spiritual practices are designed for our good to connect us to God, self, and others through loving attachment, which leads to the abundant life Jesus promised.

So how do we, and those we lead, engage in spiritual practices in each relational space to grow in loving attachment to God, self, and others?

Practices for Divine Space

Before we address spiritual practices in this space, it's important to note that every place is a space God already indwells. As the psalmist rhetorically asks in Psalm 139, "Where can I go from your Spirit? Where can I flee from your presence?" The answer is nowhere. God is with us everywhere we go. We might "leave" God, but God never leaves us. Our practices in this space are meant to enable us to be present with God and self in every other space.

So what are those practices, and how do we help people engage in them effectively? Let's harken back to the disciple-making process and remember that making disciples who grow up into maturity requires that we acknowledge that everyone starts the journey as spiritual infants. And what do infants need? They need nurture, and they need milk. Spiritual infants need to feed on the Word of God. To attach to God, we need to know who God is, what God does, and what God's voice sounds like. We need to teach disciples to read the Bible with a desire to renew their minds, feed their souls, and attune their ears to God's voice.[4] The best way to discern a person's voice is to become familiar with that person and the kinds of things that person says. But reading the Bible does not in itself guarantee attachment to God's love and attunement to God's voice.

Jesus confronted the religious leaders in John 5:39-40 by saying, "You study the Scriptures diligently because you think that in them you have eternal life. These are the very Scriptures that testify about me, yet you refuse to come to me to have life." These leaders knew the Scriptures as good as anyone, yet they didn't know God. In fact, Jesus says this of them in John 5:37-38: "You have never heard his voice nor seen his form, nor does his word dwell in you, for you do not believe the one he sent (referring to himself)." According to Jesus, you can be the best student of the Bible, reading it regularly, and still not know God. You can have a relationship with the Bible and never have a relationship with the God of the Bible. This should bring a sobriety to any spiritual leader or teacher. It's possible for us to lead and teach people to know the Bible while personally remaining disconnected from God.

We need to teach disciples not just to know the Bible but to meet with God as they read or listen to Scripture. This requires asking the same Spirit who inspired the Scriptures to speak to them through the Scriptures. I have found that the best way to do this is to teach people to ask the Spirit to speak as they read or listen to Scripture, write down what they hear, test it according to the rest of Scripture, and respond to God in prayer.

For this to happen, a new follower of Jesus will need to learn how to engage in this space by being with another more-seasoned Christian to help them practice. As they grow, they will be able to engage in listening to God through his Word on their own.

A new follower is born again by hearing and believing the Word, then they grow up by listening to God through the Scriptures. A new disciple, just like a young child learning to talk, also must learn to use their own voice to grow in their relationship with God. Prayer is essential to loving attachment and spiritual vitality. We need to learn to give voice to the cry of our hearts to bring our true self before God. The Psalms are a great place to train new followers of Jesus to give voice to their heart's cry.[5]

Sadly, far too many new Christians think they must pray in a certain way and sound like other Christians for their prayers to be heard. But Jesus said the way to enter the Kingdom of Heaven is to become like a little child. What do little children do? They give voice to their feelings and needs, no matter how messy their thoughts and words are. They aren't afraid to say exactly what they are thinking or believing, even if it might be wrong. The Psalms show us the same thing. One of the best ways to show new Christians how to pray is to teach them to personalize a psalm by putting it into their own words. Then teach them to write their own prayers in a journal and give voice to them as they speak to God.

If you read most of the personal psalms, you will notice a pattern. Most start off with the psalmist telling the truth about where he is and what he is going through. Often, it's very messy and not always truthful about God or even the world. However, in most cases the psalmist is brought back around by the Spirit to what is true.[6] It is this practice of prayer that both speaks to God and listens for God to speak that develops attachment through prayer. An example of this kind of praying can also be seen in the Emmanuel Prayer ("God is with us" prayer) developed by Jim Wilder.[7]

Silence and solitude are also significant practices that help us to engage with ourselves and God to form attachment. In silence, we learn to shut off external sources of noise to let the internal cries of our soul be heard. Far too often we try to drown out the voice of our hearts by immersing ourselves in an unending cacophony of noise via our devices. People need to learn to turn off these other sources to make space for the cry of their hearts to be noticed. Sometimes the best way to practice this is in solitude. The goal is to make space for your true self to emerge and then, as you show up more fully, bring your true self, just as you are, to God. This is a practice that might only be able to be done for a short time at first, but with ongoing practice it can grow from a few minutes to a few hours to a whole day.[8]

We won't learn to attach to God if the true self is hidden under layers of activity and noise. Most of us have practiced hiding and running away from God through performance, workaholism, or busying ourselves with multiple distractions. The practice of silence and solitude teaches us to see and embrace who we really are, knowing God already loves us just as we are. God doesn't love our future self more than our present self. God loves you right now as much as he will ever love you.[9]

There are other practices to engage in to develop attachment to God such as fasting, where we learn to hunger for God more than food, and sabbath, where we learn to rest in God, who is always working even when we don't see it. The goal in any practice of abstinence (silence, solitude, fasting, and sabbath) is to remove something in order to make more space for God and self to attach.[10]

Practices for Transparent Space

We also need to engage in spiritual practices with those who know us best. One of those practices is the Daily Examen. This is a practice we can train people to do on their own (as a practice for divine space), but it is also very helpful to share what we discover with others.

Begin by taking time to be aware of God's presence, inviting the Spirit to lead your review of the day by highlighting whatever God wants you to be aware of and present with. Then, take time to give thanks for all that you are grateful for today. Next, invite the Spirit to make you aware of the feelings you experienced throughout the day, as well as the feelings you have as you engage in this process. Those feelings are meant to make you aware of your need for God.[11] Bring those needs to God, inviting God to give you what you need. As you review the day, with the Spirit's help, acknowledge any way in which you fell short and need to receive God's grace. Then, invite the Spirit to help you look forward to tomorrow and give you direction for how to approach the next day. Commit to God in prayer whatever the Spirit shows you.

Why is the Examen included as part of the transparent space? Because this daily practice will significantly shape our time with those closest to us. In fact, this practice may be best learned by doing it with a few others and sharing aloud what we are thankful for, what we feel, what we want or need, and where we need God's kindness and grace for where we have fallen short.

When training people to engage in this space, we need to equip them in the practices of attunement to the Spirit and self, giving thanks, confession, profession, and surrender. The practice of attunement was already addressed in the content around silence and solitude. Giving thanks is often overlooked, as people are prone to talk first about what is wrong with their lives. The practice of giving thanks is not limited to one space. However, our transparent space is a great way to remind one another to give thanks in all circumstances. When we give thanks, the brain releases serotonin and dopamine. We now know that it is impossible to experience anxiety while also giving thanks.

Confession, profession, and surrender are three core practices to engage in here.[12] When we confess, we speak out to others what is inside us. We confess our feelings, our doubts, our fears, our sins, our needs, our desires, and our hopes. Sometimes the best way to respond to someone who is confessing is simply to acknowledge that we hear them and that what they are going through sounds painful, scary, or sad. The goal is not to fix people. That is the Spirit's role. The goal is to be present with one another.[13]

I have found that asking people what they want or need is more important at this point than trying to solve their problems. Our role is to help people express out loud what they are going through, what they want and need, and, with the help of the Spirit, to trust that God will meet them and direct them forward. As we engage in this process, we may have the opportunity to help others profess out loud what they do know to be true about God and themselves. Most often the Spirit will remind them of what is true, and then we can affirm that this truly is from God. There are times in this space where we need to bring what is true in order to correct a person who is believing lies. This whole process can result in practicing surrender as we collectively submit to God in prayer what we are experiencing.[14]

Few Christians have space to practice confession with people who truly know their story and care deeply for their soul. I am learning that neglecting this space may be one of the greatest reasons so few people experience significant transformation. In the absence of having safe or skilled people to practice this with, many seek out spiritual directors. I have found a spiritual director to be very helpful in my life. And yet, a healthy disciple-making community needs to equip people to engage in these practices with people who do life together as well.

Practices for Personal Space

The words *one another* are used 100 times in 94 verses in the Bible. The key themes of these "one another" practices are unity, love, and humility. The "one anothers" we need to equip disciples of Jesus to engage in are: being devoted to one another, bearing with one another, tolerating one another, forgiving one another, submitting to one another, rejoicing with one another, weeping with one another, teaching and admonishing one another, serving one another, encouraging one another, spurring one another on to love and good deeds, regarding one another as more important than yourself, and praying for one another, to name a few.

We need to engage in these "one anothers" in every space, but smaller groups are likely the best space to grow in them. Many ministries have little opportunity for people to develop in these practices because their disciple-making spaces are limited to public gatherings and alone time with God. We need to create the space for people to live out the "one another" commands. I've found that it is also in this personal space where the "one anothers" are most often needed, as our true selves tend to show up in the space where we are doing life together in community.

One of the key practices we can grow in as we engage in these "one anothers" is practicing feasting together. It is often through sharing a meal that our need for the "one anothers" comes to the surface. People let down their guard while sharing a meal or a drink together. Sharing a common meal connects us at the place of common need. We are hungry or thirsty together and also having that need met together. When this happens, our physical experience of eating or drinking creates a communal connection. This often helps us drop our guard and share the more relational, emotional, and spiritual needs we have.

A good practice to engage in when this happens is what some call "high/low." In the microchurch I presently lead, we start by sharing a common meal to which every member contributes. After we've eaten, we ask people whether they want to share what they are celebrating (high) or where they are struggling (low). They are welcome to share both if they'd like. This leads us to rejoice with those who rejoice and weep with those who weep. It is through this practice that we also learn to bear one another's burdens. We usually pray for one another in response to the needs we make known. In a very short time that is simple to facilitate, disciples practice feasting together, rejoicing and weeping together, bearing with one another, regarding one another as more important (as we take the time to be present and listen to someone else), encouraging one another, and praying for one another. Through this process, we often end up serving one another when a need is made known.

Paul instructs the church in Corinth that when they get together, they are also to teach and admonish one another as each one contributes.[15] Some of the practices he encourages us to engage in are singing to one another, bringing an instruction, and sharing a word of knowledge or prophecy. These aren't prescriptive, but they *are examples* of some of the many ways we can build one another up as we each come together prepared to contribute. The goal of these and other practices in personal space is to help people attach to God and one another in order to grow up more and more in the likeness of Christ.

Practices for Social Space

As people grow in love for one another in their personal spaces (small groups), we need to encourage, equip, and lead them to create social space for others not yet in the family of God so they too can experience the love of God in community.

I often use the example of fostering to adopt as a description of what we are aiming to do in this space. Anyone familiar with foster care will recognize this analogy. Families who are engaged in caring for foster children (and whose goal is to adopt) want to help a foster child feel like they truly belong to the family. They aim to treat this child like they would their own. And their hope is that the child will feel so loved and cared for that they will want to be a part of a loving family as well. Sometimes the foster child is able to return to their biological family, assuming that family has become a safe and loving place. However, if there is no safe and loving home to return to, the foster family hopes that a judge will decide that the foster child is best cared for by being adopted legally into this new family.

God's people are called to this same spiritual practice of hospitality. At the heart, hospitality is making space for the stranger to be at home with God through God's people. Gospel-informed hospitality creates space for the outsider or stranger to experience the loving welcome of God without any need to change or conform. Just as God demonstrated his love for us while we were still sinners, strangers, and enemies, God calls his children to do the same.

Through hospitality we create space for people to be, to be at rest, to be known, to be loved, and to become who they were always meant to be. The practice of hospitality creates space for people to be who they truly are in the midst of a loving community without any need to change in order to be loved and accepted. This creates a space for people to truly rest from performing, pretending, and striving. As people feel free to drop their veil, they experience being truly known and loved for who they really are. This leads them to make their needs known and experience a loving community that cares for them well. Over time, the Spirit works in these spaces to bring true transformation as people meet Jesus through his people and learn to entrust their lives to him and to others.

Practices for Public Space

Most churches and ministries already have this space in place. However, the question we need to ask is: How well are we leading people to attach to God and others through this space?

If the public spaces we create are primarily a performance with people on a stage as the actors and the people in the seats as observers, then we are missing the point altogether. The goal of our larger gatherings is to teach, model, and lead people to know and experience the spiritual practices in such a way that they will move toward practicing them in the other spaces. This is the goal of liturgy. *Liturgy* literally means "the work of or for the people." The goal of liturgy is to lead people through experiential practices that inform and equip them to engage in these same practices in daily life.

Think about your liturgy. Some of you are saying, "We're not really a liturgical church." You might not fit the category of "liturgical" in your mind, but any order of service is a liturgy. What does your liturgy inform and equip your people to do? Is it telling them they are primarily observers or consumers? Or is it leading them to be worshipers in all of life who are growing in their attachment love with God and others?

Some examples of the spiritual practices we can engage in through our liturgies are: the call to worship, greeting one another, singing, giving thanks, confession, hearing God's Word, receiving instruction, engaging in reflection, practicing silence, remembering Christ through the Jesus Meal, giving, receiving a blessing, and being commissioned to be on mission.

At Doxa Church, where I previously served, we taught disciples how to engage the liturgy for their own equipping. We explained that the call to worship was meant to equip them to start every day in the posture of worship and dependency on God. The greeting time was meant to equip them in how to reach out to and welcome others. Our time of singing was meant to train them to regularly speak or sing words that are true of God to one another throughout the week. Giving thanks was designed to train people to learn to be content in every circumstance. Confession was designed to show them how they can let what is inside come out in divine space, transparent space, and (where appropriate) personal space. Hearing God's Word was meant to teach them to value the Scriptures and to learn to submit themselves to God's Word in their lives. Receiving instruction from a skilled teacher was designed to equip everyone to both receive God's instruction from others and to become equipped to teach God's Word themselves. The times we create for silence and reflection were intended to shape the space they created daily for similar silence and reflection. The Jesus Meal was given to us by Jesus to remind us of what he has done but also to equip us to share that same good news with others and to learn to remember Jesus at every meal. At Doxa, we intentionally trained people to learn how to share the good news of Jesus through the Meal.[16] Our time of giving was meant to develop disciples in the practice of generosity. The benediction was designed to show believers that they are to not just give but also receive from others. And lastly, the commission to mission at the end of the gathering was a reminder both to be on mission in our social spaces and to be empowered by the Spirit and the presence of Christ in every moment for his mission.

All these spaces are ripe with opportunity to lead people to lovingly attach to God and others. How well are you stewarding them? Which practices do you need to better equip disciples with?

NOTES

1. Matthew 16:24 (New Living Translation)
2. John 17:3
3. John 17:20-26
4. Years ago, I was interacting with some leaders who wrote a book to help disciples multiply disciples. I asked one of the leaders how many people in his context could read. He said the majority were illiterate, and as he did, he put his head into his hands, discouraged as he recognized that the means they had embraced was a literate form (a book). As we processed the problem, we talked about the need to develop oral forms of learning God's Word. Keep that in mind as you think about your context and the importance of using oral forms of development.
5. The Jesus Prayer that he taught his disciples to pray in Matthew 6:9-13 is also key in training for prayer.
6. Psalm 22 is a great example of this. It is also the prayer Jesus cried out from the cross.
7. The Emmanuel prayer leads people through a guided prayer time where they invite the Spirit to help them to be present with their awareness of God's awareness of them. The process leads people to respond to some statements as though God were making them. The first statement is "I can see you," which leads the participant to write out what God sees as he observes them. Things like "I can see you drinking coffee," "I can see your heart beating quickly," or "I see you sitting in your favorite chair." The next statement is "I can hear you," which leads the participant to write down what God hears going on in their heart and mind. Then they state, "I can see how big or hard this is for you" as they go on to describe God saying that he sees how painful, scary, or difficult the situation is. The next statement is "I am glad to be with you and show sympathy and compassion for what you are going through" as the person receives God's kindness and loving presence. Lastly, the participant hears, "I can do something about what you are going through" as they are led by the Spirit to write down what God says to their situation.
8. Ruth Haley Barton's book *Invitation to Solitude and Silence: Experiencing God's Transforming Presence* is also very helpful.
9. David J. Benner's works, *Surrender to Love* and *The Gift of Being Yourself*, are helpful works in this process.
10. *Disciplines for the Inner Life* by Bob Benson and Michael W. Benson is a helpful tool; John Mark Comer's *Practicing the Way* resources are also very helpful.
11. Voice of the Heart by Chip Dodd and The Voice of the Heart Bible Study by Jeff Schulte and Phil Herndon are great tools to grow in becoming aware of your emotions; *Untangling Emotions* by J. Alasdair Groves and Winston T. Smith is also helpful; *Gospel Through the Heart—Feeling Your Way to Jesus* by Jeff Vanderstelt and Jeff Schulte, available in 2024, is another helpful tool.
12. We will practice these in our personal space as well, but most need to learn in their safe transparent space.
13. Remember Job's friends. At first, they did this well. Then they tried to play god in Job's life and stepped too far.

14. Saturatetheworld.com has some great resources to shape this space (DNA groups and Triads); Eden Project also provides some very helpful resources for triads to practice this together.

15. 1 Corinthians 14:26-33

16. If you want to learn how to grow in sharing Jesus over the Jesus meal (communion or The Lord's Supper), consider the resource we created at saturatetheworld.com.

✻ Invite Kayla . . .

CHAPTER NINE
Planning Intentional Spaces

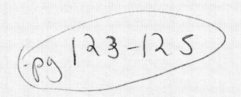

pg 123-125

Start with an Assessment

Think about your present context. How intentional are you
about creating relational spaces for disciple-making, and how
equipped are your people to engage them for the purpose of
attaching to God and others?

We intentionally create relational spaces for disciple-making.

    1   2   3   4   5   6   7   8   9   10

Our people are well-equipped to engage these spaces.

    1   2   3   4   5   6   7   8   9   10

These spaces effectively lead to relational attachment.

    1   2   3   4   5   6   7   8   9   10

Our people are well-equipped in the spiritual practices.

    1   2   3   4   5   6   7   8   9   10

Which of the relational spaces are missing or need more attention?

Which of the practices are missing or need more equipping?

What needs the most attention in our present context?

What do we already have in place that works but needs some adjustments?

What adjustments could be made to lead to more effective relational attachment?

DESIGNING INTENTIONAL SPACES

Consider the big picture. What spaces exist? What spaces need to exist? And which spiritual practices do we want to see people engaging in each of the spaces?

Take some time to build out your ideal reality as you consider your context.

Divine Space

Where do we presently want people to engage in this space?

Which practices do we equip people to engage in here and how?

Surrender - time alone w/ God in nature.

What do we need to add, subtract, or change?

Transparent Space

Where do we want people to engage in this space?

1-2 ppl close enough w/?

Which practices do we equip people to engage in here and how?

vunerable, true self

What do we need to add, subtract, or change?

*More time together.

* Group that challenges you - not makes you 100% comfortable - Janet, Greic, Kat..

Personal Space
Where do we want people to engage in this space?

Which practices do we equip people to engage in here and how?

What do we need to add, subtract, or change?

Social Space
Where do we want people to engage in this space?

Which practices do we equip people to engage in here and how?

What do we need to add, subtract, or change?

Public Space

[handwritten: Real authentic relationships.]
*[handwritten: *Not just job or career but ministry/ mission station—work secondary—]*

How do our public gatherings equip people for the practices?

*[handwritten: *Bible study, work, Zumba class,]*

[handwritten: Primary Sharing Jesus.]

What do we need to add, subtract, or change?

How might we redesign this space for more effective equipping?

Next Steps

What can we do in the next 90 days to begin to implement necessary changes?

What will we do in the next 6 months?

What will we do in the next year?

FROM STRIVING TO THRIVING

FROM STRIVING TO THRIVING

At the time of this writing, I have had the privilege, joy, and pain of serving the Church in some form for 33 years. I have led, taught, equipped, and watched people of all ages aim to follow Jesus, obey his commands, and make disciples of Jesus, who did the same.

I have also watched people get burned out, worn out, used, and discarded. I know of far too many people who are disillusioned with the Church and in many cases have abandoned the faith altogether. I have worked under very toxic, unhealthy leaders and sadly have contributed as a leader myself to toxic culture and unhealth.

I have run out of hands and fingers to count all the leaders who have fallen, blown up, and even lost their own lives in this work. Frankly, I am tired of it and have enough healthy anger in me to not just sit by and watch it continue. I have been doing my own work to get healthy the past four years and am committed to help others as well.

For the sake of the gospel and a lost world who may be open to Jesus but isn't sure about his family, the Church, we must make a shift from striving to thriving. We need disciples who walk in step with and are empowered by the Spirit, and we need leaders who are emotionally, relationally, and spiritually healthy, who can also create culture that breeds greater emotional, relational, and spiritual health.

CHAPTER TEN

Spirit-Empowered Ministry

Working in Our Own Strength

When we first started to form a core for the church that would be known as Soma in Tacoma, Washington, I called people to follow Jesus and walk in his ways, doing what he did and commanded. People were inspired and motivated and eager to practice and implement all that I was teaching. But it didn't take long before people started to express being overwhelmed or worn out. We had made a fatal mistake. We had called them to do the work of Jesus without the power and presence of Jesus by the Spirit.

Jesus was very clear about this. He told his disciples that apart from him they could do nothing.[1] When he gave them the commission to make disciples of all nations, he promised them his power and presence to be with them as they journeyed on his mission.[2] In fact, he told them before he ascended to wait for power from on high, referring to the Spirit anointing, filling, and empowering them to be his witnesses.[3]

I wonder how many of us are calling people to do the work of Jesus without the presence and power of the Holy Spirit? How many of us are trying to lead without his presence and power?

Empowered by Love

When Jesus started his public ministry, he began in the waters of baptism with John the Baptist. Jesus didn't need to be baptized for repentance and the removal of sin. Jesus was baptized to identify with us and our common need for God. We, like Jesus, need power from on high. Jesus was baptized in the Jordan, the same river God had dried up for the Israelites to pass into the Promised Land. They had witnessed God's power repeatedly, and even here, they could see and remember that it was by God's power that they entered into their new life. And yet, they quickly slipped back into self-sufficiency mode. Jesus entered his ministry not just setting an example of full submission and dependency on God, but also doing for God's people what they failed to do themselves. And when Jesus came out of the waters of baptism, the Holy Spirit descended upon him in bodily form like a dove, and Jesus heard the Father say, "You are my Son, whom I love; with you I am well pleased."[4]

Jesus began his ministry in a place of dependency so that he could receive the anointing of the Spirit. He also did not engage in ministry to gain the Father's approval. He started with a full tank of affection. He had all the power and all the love to go forward in ministry.

Do the people you lead know the voice of God speaking to them by the Spirit, affirming that they are unbelievably loved by the Father?[5] If not, they will believe they have to earn God's love by doing all that Jesus did. But remember, the

Father expressed his love for the Son before his ministry even began. We need to teach and remind disciples that they are doing the work of Jesus not to gain love but from a place of the fullness of God's love.

I went through a hard season where God called me to cease from all ministry in the form of a sabbatical. My spiritual director showed me that getting off the horse of ministry wouldn't be enough. He informed me that my temptation would be to get on a different horse of accomplishment. He helped me to identify every horse of accomplishment that might be a temptation for me. I began to make a list: losing weight, putting on more muscle, improving my golf game, reading more books, doing some writing, etc. He gently admonished me to not get on any horses until I could stay on the horse of rest and know I was still deeply loved by God regardless of any accomplishment (or lack thereof).

I must admit, it was one of the hardest seasons of my life. I had become so accustomed to my sense of approval and love coming from what I did (even though I regularly taught that we were loved apart from works) that I began to realize that I didn't love myself apart from what I accomplished. This revealed that I didn't fully embrace God's love for me without my works. I sat in this for many weeks. One day I took a walk for five hours, and while I sat on a bench looking out on the Puget Sound, I sensed the Father's love for me so deeply that I was brought to the same place that I imagine Jesus was at in that river. I knew, I really knew, that God really loved me, even if I never did another thing for him again.

When I recount this experience, I often say that it was that day that I made a shift from ambition to affection. I had been operating from a place of ambition, which seeks to gain what one doesn't yet have. Now I am learning to operate from a place of affection, which recognizes I already have everything I need in the love of God. I am working from fullness of love, not an attempt to gain it. As I write these words, my heart is overwhelmed, and my eyes are full of tears as I remember that moment when God poured fresh fountains of love into my being. This is the place we all need to be working from—the overflow of God's love.

Are we leading from that place? Are we leading others to continually be filled with the Holy Spirit, and are we experiencing the neverending flow of God's love into our hearts? In Ephesians 5:18, Paul exhorts us to not be drunk with wine but to be filled (continually) with the Holy Spirit. I don't think Paul's main concern is drinking here (though we are wise to heed his exhortation about not getting drunk). I believe Paul is saying, "Don't depend on anything else for healing, for filling, for empowering than the Holy Spirit. And just like you know how to drink liquid, drink in the Holy Spirit continually."

Empowered to Overcome

Luke 4 tells us that Jesus was filled with the Spirit and led by the Spirit to go into the wilderness, and it was there that he was tempted by the devil. I've heard many people ask, "How did Jesus overcome the temptation?" And most respond, "By the Word of God," referring to Jesus quoting Scripture. The only problem with this answer is that the devil was also quoting Scripture to tempt Jesus. In fact, I've sadly observed many people use Scripture to tempt people to sin and even justify their own sin.

Scripture alone is not what empowered Jesus to overcome temptation. Yes, the Scriptures informed Jesus, but they alone did not empower Jesus to overcome. Jesus overcame temptation by resting in the Father's love, knowing the Scriptures, and being filled by the Spirit. Luke doesn't want us to miss this. In fact, that is what Luke is making clear in his second book, the Acts of the Apostles. (I wonder if we should call it the "Works of Jesus Through His People Empowered by His Spirit"? Maybe too long?) As a meticulous historian, Luke records how Jesus continued to build his Church, empowering his followers to stand up in the face of temptation and persecution because they had been with Jesus, knew they were loved, and were also filled and empowered with his presence by His Spirit.

Empowered to Preach

The next thing Luke records Jesus doing is returning to Galilee "filled with the power of the Spirit," teaching in the synagogues. On one occasion, recorded in Luke 4, Jesus went to Nazareth, his hometown. He entered the synagogue and opened the scroll to Isaiah 61, where he read, "'The Spirit of the Lord is on me, because he has anointed me to proclaim good news to the poor. He has sent me to proclaim freedom for the prisoners and recovery of sight for the blind, to set the oppressed free, to proclaim the year of the Lord's favor.'" Jesus rolled up the scroll, handed it to the attendant, and sat down. Everyone was staring at Jesus, and he said, "Today this Scripture is fulfilled in your hearing," referring to himself. The people were amazed at Jesus' gracious words, and they asked, "Isn't this Joseph's son?" There are two important things they are saying without saying them. One, which is more obvious, "How can Joseph's son be the Messiah?" The other is, "How did Jesus, who we have known since he was a little tyke, speak like this?" Luke wants us to see that Jesus was able to do so because he was filled and anointed with the Holy Spirit. This same phenomenon occurs when Jesus-followers are anointed and filled with the Holy Spirit after he ascends. They all, like Jesus, are empowered to preach. The same is true for every disciple. As Jesus said himself in John 14:12, "Whoever believes in me will do the works I have been doing."

Do the disciples around you know this? Do they know they can be empowered to speak the gospel like Jesus was empowered to preach? If not, they will strive in their own power to try and come up with their own persuasive words instead of receiving power and the words to speak from the Holy Spirit.

Empowered for the Miraculous

After this, Luke records Jesus casting out demons, healing many people, continuing to preach with power and authority, and eventually calling his disciples. Once again, in his second book, Luke records the followers of Jesus doing the same. Jesus had promised that those who believed in him would also do what Jesus did by the power of the same Spirit who enabled him. They cast out demons, they healed, they preached the good news, and they made many disciples. And this wasn't done by just the twelve. As we continue reading, when persecution broke out in Jerusalem, the twelve stayed there, but all the other disciples were driven out of Jerusalem, and they preached the good news wherever they went.

Is this what we are experiencing today? Are you witnessing this same kind of power in the people God has given you to influence and lead? Or are we calling people to try and do the works of Jesus without the same power he had?

I am increasingly convinced that the reason so many of us see so little work that looks like Jesus is because we are trying to do what Jesus did without Jesus and without his Spirit to empower us.

Naturally Supernatural

I have a couple of dear friends who are gifted by God to help the Church have a very different experience with the Spirit. Alex and Hannah Absalom lead a ministry called Dandelion Resourcing.[6] One of the things they teach is what they call being "naturally supernatural." They recognize that many followers of Jesus are ill-equipped in being filled with the presence and power of the Holy Spirit. They believe it ought to be natural for a disciple of Jesus to not only be filled with the Spirit but also participating with the Spirit to see and experience the same things Jesus did. Some of us have a lot of fear around this either because we have been taught to fear it or we have observed or experienced abuse. They do such a great job of leading people in ways that feel safe and normative, not scary and weird.

I know there are different views on this, and yet I would challenge us all to let the Holy Spirit speak through the Scriptures. The Bible alone does not empower a follower of Jesus to do what Jesus did. The Bible informs and gives us great courage and clarity, but without the power of the Spirit we can do nothing. Paul is clear about this when discussing our salvation. He exhorts us to work out our salvation with fear and trembling, "For God (by the Spirit) is working in you, giving you the desire and the power to do what pleases him."[7]

Think back on all you've read so far. Think about the *definition* of a disciple: one who is committed to be with Jesus, to become like Jesus, and to do what Jesus did and is doing. These things are impossible apart from the Spirit. Think about the process of making a mature disciple: going from spiritually dead to infant, child, young adult, and spiritual parent. Impossible apart from the Spirit. Now, think about the process of D.E.E.P.E.R. equipping. Where are disciples seeing how to be filled and empowered by the Holy Spirit for the same works Jesus did and is doing? What experiences are disciples engaging in themselves? Who's explaining how to be filled, led, and empowered by the Spirit? Where can they practice stepping out into the works the Spirit brings about? Is there a safe place to try and fail without being called crazy or a heretic? Jesus certainly gave space for his disciples to be exposed in gentle ways. And is there a place to reflect on their experience and to process what they believe and what they need to still learn and grow in?

We are commanded by Jesus to make disciples and teach them to obey everything he commanded. That includes being filled, led, and empowered by the Spirit to do the same works Jesus did.

Is this happening in your present context? What needs to change? What next steps will you take?

Empowered at Soma

When we started to make this more "normal" for the disciples who were part of Soma, God granted us many opportunities. One of my favorite stories is about my friend Clay, who had never been part of a church and who came to faith in Jesus through our missional community.[8] Once he came to believe in and follow Jesus, Clay and I had many conversations about how the Spirit would now empower him to do the same things

Jesus did. I remember him saying to me, "Jeff, I hope you don't expect me to preach the gospel to others like you did to me." I kept informing him that the Spirit would empower him just like the Spirit empowered me.

In the coming days, Clay found out that he had a tumor that had grown around his spinal cord. He was told that the surgery might take away his ability to walk. In light of this, Clay went on a surfing trip, knowing it could be his last. Clay also asked us to pray for his healing, and we did. During surgery, when they opened up Clay's back, the tumor was gone! God had healed him. We came into the hospital room to celebrate with Clay, but he was sleeping when we arrived. The guy in the bed next to Clay asked us, "Who is your friend? Is he some kind of preacher or something?" When we asked why he would ask that, he said, "Well, he's been telling me about Jesus and how he healed him and how he can heal me too." We all laughed and then agreed with what Clay had said. "It's true. He can." I reflected on how Clay didn't think he could share Jesus, and here he was declaring to a stranger Jesus' power to heal.

Time passed, and I watched Clay drift a bit in his interest and engagement, as I've seen many new Christians do. I was praying for him one morning while driving home from an early morning meeting at our local coffee shop. All of a sudden, a group of fire trucks and ambulances sped past me. I noticed they were turning down the road Clay lived on, so I followed them and started to feel a lot of fear when I saw Clay's wife, Kristi, outside crying. I parked the car and ran over to her, hugged her, and asked, "Is Clay all right?" She said, "Yes," as she pointed across the street. "He's right there."

Eventually Clay joined us and shared what had happened.

The man across the street had hung himself in his garage, and his girlfriend had come outside screaming. Clay was just walking out to bring his daughter to school at the same time. Clay ran into the garage and tried to get the man down, but it felt like he weighed 800 pounds. Clay shared that he didn't know what to do and started praying. Then he saw a pair of scissors in the corner. He cut the rope and lowered the man down. There was no pulse and no breathing. So he administered CPR for a while ... still nothing. He was gone.

Clay stepped back and prayed one more time. "If it's his time to go, Father, take him home. If not, in the name of Jesus, bring him back to life!" At that moment, Clay felt some power come into the room, and the man started breathing again. He was alive!

This reignited Clay's walk with God—how could it not? I remember him sharing with another man from Soma, "I wonder if God is trying to show me that I am supposed to start reaching out to my neighbors more?"

Is it possible that so many people have developed hard hearts and a cold faith because they have been striving to live the life of a disciple all in their own power? Maybe they need a fresh wind and fire from the Spirit to awaken their hearts and reignite their faith. Maybe you do too.

What steps will you take to walk in the Spirit? What needs to change for you to lead and train others to do the same in your context?

NOTES

1. John 15
2. Matthew 28:18-20
3. Acts 1:4-8
4. Luke 3:21-22
5. See Romans 5:5, 8; 8:12-17, 31-39
6. See https://www.dandelionresourcing.com.
7. Philippians 2:13
8. You can hear more from Clay and our missional community in this video: https://www.youtube.com/watch?v=kxviBBxbZqI&t=31s.

CHAPTER ELEVEN

Your Relational Journey

Hitting the Wall

Just prior to COVID-19 breaking out, I hit a wall. I had been in some form of vocational ministry for 29 years at that point, and my brain and my body couldn't stay silent any longer.

Your brain and body are a gift that way. They do help you get through difficult and traumatic times and survive, but they will also tell you when it's too much, and, if necessary, bring you to a halting stop so you will take care of yourself.[1]

In the few years prior, there were cracks forming and warning signs flashing. The breaking point came when my best friend and son in the faith, Randy Sheets, took his own life on November 14, 2019.[2] He had been the man I poured my life into. He and his wife were best friends to Jayne and me. In many ways, he was one of the best examples of a disciple who became a spiritual parent I could point to from my own life and ministry. He and Lisa had lived with us during their first year of marriage. I had not only discipled him but mentored him into his leadership role, where I eventually handed to him the baton of leading Soma Church in Tacoma as I prepared to move and lead a church replant in Bellevue.

In the fall of 2014, I had been asked to consider stepping into what had been the live preaching campus of Mars Hill in Bellevue and to restart a church. Most of the other Mars Hill campuses had a campus pastor who could step up and lead the campus to become a new congregation. Bellevue Mars Hill, however, had been the epicenter of the explosion, and, along with Mark Driscoll and the campus pastor, 15 of the 18 elders had left. After a significant time of prayerful discernment with the Soma Tacoma elders and many other leaders at Soma, we believed God was calling Jayne and I to move to Bellevue and replant the church. In January of 2015, we began to lead Doxa Church. Mars Hill Sammamish joined us as well, which brought a few other elders to the team.

Many of my ministry peers around the country could not believe I would do this. Some were dumbfounded because our models of ministry were so radically different. This seemed like a hard left turn to them. One person, in fact, told me this would be ministry suicide, as I would lose much of my credibility because it appeared like a departure from what I had taught for so long. Some, sadly, thought we should let the church die, to which I argued that just because most of the shepherds left the sheep, we don't justify leaving the sheep shepherd-less. Others who were watching from afar shared later that they were concerned for my own emotional and relational well-being. I remember one leader from Mars Hill

Bellevue, who eventually became an elder at Doxa, asked me during one of the interviews, "Why in the world would you ever come and take this job?" I think he was concerned that I was either crazy or didn't really know what I was stepping into. It turns out both were true.

I recently recorded a podcast with Chuck DeGroat, author of *When Narcissism Comes to Church*. I shared with him that I was terribly naïve when I stepped into the job in Bellevue—naïve about how difficult and painful the work would be and naïve about my own emotional unhealth, which would make it even harder. I remarked that, had I known more about both, I would have called him and a few others[3] in to assess both the culture of the church and my own emotional health as well. I still believe we were supposed to step into that work, and I affirm that God brought about some very beautiful redemption and restoration in both the church and my own heart. But who steps into something like that? In my case, someone who has a rescuer mentality and savior complex, and someone who also feels at home in spiritually broken or abusive situations.

Have you ever stopped and considered where you've ended up and why? Do you know your heart's motives for why you're doing what you do? Have you taken time to consider what has shaped you and how you've responded to it?

What Shaped Us

I grew up very involved in the church. My parents were volunteer youth leaders when I was a child. We went to church gatherings at least two times on Sunday and once on Wednesday. When I became a teenager, I joined our youth choir and drama team, and I was very involved in our youth ministry. Our senior pastor was in charge of it all. He had a large capacity to do a lot and a very controlling presence as well. Before I hit my wall and began doing my work, I had rose-colored glasses about my childhood and our church.[4] Today, I see that shame and fear were used to motivate or manipulate many of our behaviors there.

I remember many times where I or someone else in the church was publicly shamed to make the point that you don't also want to fail and be found out. When I was 12, while at a youth conference for a weekend, I was late to a meeting because I got lost. Our pastor called me out in front of 60 or more junior high and high school students and then sent me to my room for the whole night to write Scripture verses for four hours while everyone else enjoyed the activities. Thinking back on that experience, I can now see how alone and rejected I felt by a spiritual leader I trusted. It was a real wound that made a lasting impact on me.

When I was 16, my girlfriend told our youth leaders that she was pregnant. They met with me to confront me, and then they accompanied me as I shared the news with my parents. Thankfully, my parents were full of grace as my mom and dad hugged me and promised that we would walk through it together. The leadership of the church was not so gracious. Our pastor told my girlfriend and me that we would have to stand in front of the church and confess our sin publicly. They wanted to make a statement to all the other teenagers that this is what happens when you do what Jeff did. Before we were to go public, my girlfriend confessed that she made it all up. She had never been pregnant. We were both then told we no longer had to confess our sin in front of the church. Lesson learned. *Don't get caught. Learn to hide to avoid being shamed.* I did learn to hide—through religious performance in the church, athletic performance in sports, and workaholism in life. I also learned to hide by not fully showing up with what was going on inside of me.

As a teenager, I remember my dad sharing with me how he remembers this same pastor leaving his wife on the side of the road five miles from home and making her walk home because of something he believed she had done wrong. More recently I asked my mom and dad why they would entrust their teenage sons into the care of a man who would do this to his own wife. My dad said he had never really thought about how our pastor's behaviors would affect me. They did. A spiritual leader who speaks on behalf of God and uses intimidation, threats, or shame to manipulate and control behavior can deeply wound people and create very distorted pictures of what God is like. As a result of my church experience, domineering church leadership that creates cultures of fear and shame, with threats of abandonment, felt normal to me.

Looking back over the last 30 years, I can now see why I ended up serving under or alongside so many leaders who were abusive and controlling, who also created emotionally and spiritually toxic environments. It felt normal to me. And, because of that, I kept being attracted to abusive friends, leaders, and cultures. I also subconsciously wanted to rescue others. I now see that, in some cases, I contributed to the unhealth out of my own codependency. I often lost my voice out of fear, or I collaborated out of shame. I had a fear of abandonment and betrayal that went back to some of the church culture as well as from deep childhood trauma I had never dealt with. This fear had controlling power over me. My unaddressed trauma led me to overreact whenever something felt like it might lead to abandonment, betrayal, or public shame.

Think about the culture you were formed in. How did it shape you and your view of God? How are you presently leading and creating culture in light of that?

Emotionally Impaired

This all came to a head in the year and a half prior to Randy's death, and then it couldn't be ignored after he died. I am grateful that our elders gave me some time off to grieve and process Randy's death and later covered the costs for me to get help from Tin Man Ministries.[5] I met with a Tin Man coach once a week for 14 months. I also did a week-long intensive where I did a lot more work on my own story.

I discovered that I had significantly impaired my feelings and emotions. I had learned as a child that feelings were bad and not to be trusted. I belittled or diminished my feelings of sadness, hurt, loneliness, and anger. I remember sharing with my Tin Man coach about a terribly sad and painful time in my life, and he asked, "Why are you smiling? This isn't funny!" Because we were on Zoom, I could see his face and mine, and I realized in that moment that this is what I had learned to do for most of my life. I made light of my pain and sadness as though it wasn't a big deal. I had also learned to live with ongoing toxic shame. I was so harsh on myself whenever I fell short. My coach would also often tell me that I was "shoulding" on myself, as he would reflect on how often I said, "I should have done this. I shouldn't have done that."

Why am I sharing all this?

Because what happens to us happens through us.

And how we internalize what happens to us will—not might—*will* shape how we treat others, how we lead, and how we create culture. If I was shaming myself for falling short, you can be sure others were also feeling shamed by me when they fell short.

I remember asking my oldest daughter, after I had been doing some of my own work, what it had been like being on the other side of me growing up, how she experienced me. She, with a lot of courage, said, "Dad, I always believed you wouldn't be proud of me unless I was as competitive at sports as you were." Wow, that hurt! My own toxic shame had created a culture of performance in my own household, even though I regularly told my children I loved them and accepted them no matter what they did.

I now know that I had also created cultures that were not healthy in the organizations I led. And this affected others in negative ways—my family first, but also the ministries, staff, and church members I've led. Did God still work through this broken man? Yes, of course he did. And yet, God loved me enough to let me hit a wall and get help. I don't know what would have happened if I didn't. My wife and children would tell you they have a different husband and father now. My friends who have ministered with me over the years have shared that I am not the same leader. I know I have a lot of work ahead, but I am so thankful to God for his grace to get me the help I needed.

Are You Healthy?

What about you? How healthy is your leadership? How emotionally and relationally healthy are you? Ask those around you what it's like to be on the other side of you. Ask them how they experience you. If you do, prepare yourself to listen and not justify or defend yourself. It may be painful, but as I've learned these past years, if it's mentionable, it's manageable. Some of us need to hear the truth about ourselves so we can get the help we need.

The other reason this is so important is because the kind of disciples we make is shaped by the kind of leaders we are and the cultures we create. Jesus said, "Everyone who is fully trained will be like their teacher."[6] This is true of parents with their children. This is true of leaders of ministries, churches, non-profits, and businesses.

Think about your context. Consider the culture. How is the culture you lead or contribute to forming people and their view of God? Paul told Timothy, "Watch your life and doctrine closely. Persevere in them, because if you do, you will save both yourself and your hearers."[7]

When a Leader Falls

I remember preparing for a training session I was about to do with some young business leaders from Indonesia. The news about Ravi Zacharias had been made public, and the people facilitating the training mentioned before we went live that these leaders were really struggling with what to make of this news. They had revered Ravi. Now, they were confused and angry and dismayed. Sure enough, as soon as we got started, one of them asked me, "How could this happen? And do you think Ravi was even a Christian?" I said that it is not our job to answer the second question. However, I did suggest some possibilities for the first. "I didn't know Ravi personally, so what I am about to share is only conjecture."

I continued first by explaining, "All of us do what we do because of deep needs that need to be met and desires that want to be satisfied. However, some of us learned early in life to try to shut down our feelings. Maybe we were told that feelings were bad or not to be trusted. But God gave us feelings to become aware of our needs. If we feel sad, for instance, we know we need comfort. Which is why Jesus said, 'Blessed are those who mourn, for they will be comforted.'[8] Jesus knew how we were made. And he knew that if we feel our feelings, we will become aware of our needs and move toward God and others to have our needs met in healthy ways. However, if we impair our feelings (try to stuff or ignore them) and dismiss our needs, those needs and desires will often find themselves getting met in unhealthy ways. They are like the roots of an oak tree. They will break through anything to get what they need."

I continued, "Even though I didn't know Ravi and would never pretend to know his heart, I wonder whether he had experienced significant loss in his life that he never fully felt sadness over so that he could also receive the comfort he needed. If that is the case, it may be possible that his mind and body, being so needy for comfort, led him to get that comfort in inappropriate ways. I also wonder whether he had experienced significant pain in his life but dismissed it and never received the attention needed to bring deep healing.

If so, it's possible he went to inappropriate places to get attention and a false sense of healing. And maybe Ravi had been lonely as a child or young adult but wasn't free to feel that and share his need and desire to be truly seen and known. If so, it's possible that in needing to be known and wanting to be seen, he put himself in situations where he experienced a false sense of intimacy."

This conversation led us to address how these leaders were attending to their own hearts. I confessed that I had a great sense of sadness and compassion around this story. I shared with them where I had been and how I could have had a similar story told about me, had I not hit the wall and gotten the help I needed. We then proceeded to talk about feelings and how God had designed them to feel their feelings, know their needs, and go to God and others to appropriately have those needs met.

The Power of Desire

We hear James say, "When tempted, no one should say, 'God is tempting me,' for God cannot be tempted by evil, nor does he tempt anyone; but each person is tempted when they are dragged away by their own evil desire and enticed. Then, after desire has conceived, it gives birth to sin; and sin, when it is full-grown, gives birth to death."[9] You have real desires, and they are very powerful. They lure and entice. They conceive and give birth. Desires themselves are not necessarily evil. The Greek word that James uses here, which we translate as *desire*, is a neutral word, neither good nor evil, but it can lead to either. What we do know is that desires are very powerful!

Later, James asks, "What causes quarrels and what causes

fights among you? Don't they come from your desires that battle within you? You desire and do not have, so you kill. You covet but you cannot get what you want, so you quarrel and fight. You do not have because you do not ask God. When you ask, you do not receive, because you ask with wrong motives, that you may spend what you get on your pleasures."[10] James is saying that the brokenness and destruction in your life and community is caused by unattended or unmet desires inside you. Douglas J. Moo in his commentary on this passage says, "Frustrated desire is what is breeding the intense strife that is convulsing the community."

You have very real needs and desires. If you are not attending to them or are meeting them in appropriate ways, they will war within you, destroying your internal world, and they will find destructive ways to seek satisfaction that will also destroy your outside world as well.

What about you? Are you attending to your heart? Are you aware of what you need and desire? If not, do you know how to become aware of these things?

Feel Your Feelings

We become aware of our needs and desires by paying attention to what is going on inside and by feeling our feelings. One of the things I became aware of as I did my own emotional work was that I was deeply afraid of being betrayed or abandoned. Before doing my work, I had no idea this was the case. I learned over the years to ignore my fear and stuff it back down anytime it came up. I embraced the lie that good Christians have no fear. "Fear is the antithesis of faith," I subconsciously repeated to myself. Besides, the most repeated command in the Bible is "Fear not." And yet, I didn't pay attention to what comes next in this command: "for I am with you" and "for I have overcome the world."

God doesn't want us to never feel fear. God created us to feel healthy fear as an indicator when we are in danger, in the dark, or over our heads in need. Fear is meant to tell us that we need help, protection, or refuge. Fear informs us that we need God.[11] That is why Psalm 111:10 tells us that "the fear of the Lord is the beginning of wisdom." Fear tells you there is real danger. Fear tells you that you might not have all the answers. Fear, if you feel it, will lead you not just to get help and protection, but it will give you the gift of faith in someone bigger than you and wisdom to keep you from walking in the way of foolishness. That is what wisdom literature is all about. Wisdom literature instructs us to have some healthy fear and to get help and wisdom from sources we can trust.

Fear isn't the antithesis of faith. Fear makes you aware that you need to put your faith in God and others who are trustworthy.[12]

I had unfortunately learned to ignore or dismiss fear and how it was meant to lead me to get help. This impairment of my fear led me to try to control what was uncontrollable, which led to internal anxiety and external rage. I would experience anxiety when I felt out of control and then rage against anyone who would threaten my false sense of control. I wasn't a loud, external rager. In fact, in my leadership this often sounded like strategy and looked like systems and structures. But it was just my attempt to be in control of others. I've come to now understand that people could intuitively feel my rage. They didn't always feel safe around me as I tried to control my environment and others. This also led me to try and do far too much on my own. I didn't want to be seen as limited and in need of help, so I tried to become bigger than I actually was. I now see that my high capacity and my ability to get a lot of stuff done were adaptations I had learned to avoid embracing my need for God and others.

Do you know what is going on inside of you? Do you know what you're doing because of it?

Locate Yourself

When God came to Adam after he and Eve had eaten the fruit from the tree of the knowledge of good and evil, God called out, "Where are you?" God wasn't confused about where Adam was. It wasn't a GPS question. God asked this question to help Adam locate himself emotionally. Consider Adam's response in Genesis 3:10, "I heard you in the garden, and I was afraid (fear) because I was naked (shame); so I hid." Adam found himself based upon his feelings. He was feeling fear and shame. And, like me, he had impaired those feelings. If he had embraced his feeling of fear, he would not have run from God but to God for help. If he had felt healthy shame (for his own limitations), he would have recognized that he needed what God could provide—coverings of God's design, not Adam's.

So where are you? What are you feeling even as you read this? Are you regularly attending to your heart by feeling your feelings, becoming aware of your needs, and going to God and others to have those needs met in healthy ways?

What Story Informs You?

The next question God asks is: "Who told you that you were naked?" (3:11). God is going after the story they believed.

The story you were told and the story in which you live significantly shape your behaviors today. As a child, I learned that feeling fear is for wimps, and later I was taught that mature Christians should never fear. I also had come to believe early on in life that the people closest to you will abandon you or betray you, so you should do all you can to either avoid getting relationally close or aim to control people so they won't leave. Another story I believed was that it was OK for spiritual leaders to manipulate people's behaviors through shame and fear. To see these lies for what they really were, I needed help from others to unpack my story and tell me how broken and crazy it was.

What's the story you've been told? What narrative is controlling your behaviors?

What Have You Done?

The last question God asks is of the woman, "What is this you have done?" (3:13). That's the question I want to ask you as well. In light of your feelings, needs, and desires, informed by the story you have lived in and believed, what have you done in response? I over-worked, tried to live beyond my limitations, remained in isolation even though I was surrounded by people, fought for a false sense of control, raged at whatever threatened that control, shamed myself for not being or doing more, lived with ongoing fear of rejection or abandonment, and often sabotaged relationships or situations as a result.

What have you done? Or, what are you about to do?

I have had too many friends in ministry blow up their church, their family, or their own life. When I was a part of the Acts

29 network, I witnessed far too many churches implode and church planters commit suicide. Harvest Bible Chapel and Willow Creek went through terrible pain and loss. The Southern Baptist Church is losing trust because of sexual abuse that remains unproperly dealt with. We've created cultures that prop up narcissists and, in our codependency, we believe we couldn't have a fruitful ministry without them.

I'll never forget the day I heard Mark Driscoll say to me, "I am Mars Hill. I am the brand. If there is no Mark Driscoll, there is no Mars Hill." On one hand, Mark wasn't wrong. I don't think there would have been a Mars Hill without Mark. However, when one of us sees ourselves as indispensable to God's work, we are in trouble. The problem is that our culture often affirms how indispensable we are as well.[13] When I confronted the leaders of Mars Hill, sharing with them that I believed Mark was disqualified[14] and needed to take a break and get some help, they said, "We don't disagree with your concerns, but you can't argue with the fruit." They were referring to baptisms, but the Scripture tells us the fruit we are looking for is not numbers but the fruit of the Spirit. They couldn't imagine how they would continue if Mark had to step aside for a season. Sadly, for Mark and Mars Hill, the "fruit" of baptisms justified the leadership unhealth and abuse. They, like many of us, valued competency over character.

Something must change! Thousands in Seattle left the faith because of what happened at Mars Hill. I am now watching people the age of my children (Gen Z) turning away from the church because they can see how unhealthy it has become. They are interested in Jesus, just not his Church. This cannot continue without serious ramifications.

What have we done? What are we doing?

Leaders, we must repent and turn back to Jesus, the healer of our hearts. Get the help you need if you have not yet done so. Don't wait until you hit a wall. Just as we engage in preventive medicine, pursue getting emotionally healthy now.

If you are observing broken, controlling, or abusive behaviors in leadership, don't justify them by the "fruit" of numbers. If we don't make this shift from unhealth to health, from flesh-led to Spirit-empowered, from striving to thriving, we can do all we want with our disciple-making strategies but, in reality, we are only one or two generations from a dead and dying Church in North America. A younger generation has been watching and waning. They are losing trust of spiritual leaders. This loss of trust is also eroding their confidence in the message we are proclaiming. As a result, many are leaving the church and some are leaving the faith altogether. If something doesn't change in how we're leading, we may not have much left to lead.

Remember Paul's words to Timothy, "The goal of this command is love, which comes from a pure heart and a good conscience and a sincere faith."[15] Let's love God and others well by also lovingly taking care of our own emotional and spiritual health.

NOTES

1. You don't have to wait until you hit a wall to preemptively take care of yourself. Just as many do preventative health care to avoid catastrophic unhealth, I would strongly recommend you work on your emotional health now, so you don't have to hit a wall to get healthy.

2. Randy had been on three tours of duty as an Army Ranger in the Middle East. He started to experience PTSD again, combined with horrific body pain. The mix of meds, PTSD, and early childhood trauma created a dangerous cocktail that led him into a very dark space, causing him to take his life.

3. Such as Diane Langberg, author of *Redeeming Power: Understanding Authority and Abuse in the Church*, and Mindy Caliguire, a former colleague of mine when I was at Willow Creek Community Church, who now leads a ministry called Soul Care that assesses leaders and cultures for emotional, relational, and spiritual health.

4. I am not throwing the baby out with the bathwater. I do believe God was at work in my home church and that there were good people and good outcomes. I know that I also received good there. However, I have learned that it's important to tell the truth without blaming or shaming. I hope I did that well here.

5. https://www.tinmanministries.org/ I am now a Tin Man coach as well. The work was so transforming in my own life that I decided to get trained so I could help others.

6. Luke 6:40

7. 1 Timothy 4:16

8. Matthew 5:4

9. James 1:13-15

10. James 4:1-3

11. It would be wise for more leaders to have a healthy sense of fear. So much of what we do is bigger than we can handle alone. We need to cry out to God for help. We need to acknowledge when we are over our heads. We need people around us we can trust and depend on. The best leaders, like Solomon, realize they need wisdom and help from God and others. Those who pretend not to fear will create cultures of fear around them and rage at anyone who threatens their false sense of control.

12. Edward T. Welch wrote a very helpful article on this entitled "Fear Is Not Sin."

13. *A Church Called Tov—Forming a Goodness Culture that Resists Abuse of Power and Promotes Healing* by Scot McKnight and Laura Barringer is a very helpful resource. Chuck DeGroat's book, *When Narcissism Comes to Church: Healing Your Community From Emotional and Spiritual Abuse*, is also very helpful.

14. I believed Mark was disqualified for several reasons: he did not have a good reputation with outsiders. He was arrogant. He was not gentle. He was quarrelsome. He was spiritually and emotionally abusive and controlling. I discovered after I stepped into Mars Hill Bellevue that the reason they didn't use the language of disqualification was because they believed once disqualified, always disqualified. They wanted Mark to go through a process that would lead to eventual restoration. It turned out that Mark didn't trust his elders to lead him through such a process. This is evidence of a culture that did not feel safe, even to Mark, who helped to create it.

15. 1 Timothy 1:5

CHAPTER TWELVE

Changing Your Context

Start with an Assessment

Think about your present context. How Spirit-empowered
are the disciples? How important is leader health? How does
your culture breed health or unhealth? How empowered and
emotionally healthy are you?

We effectively lead and equip people for Spirit-empowered living.

     1   2   3   4   5   6   7   8   9   10

People are walking in the Spirit and empowered for ministry.

     1   2   3   4   5   6   7   8   9   10

Leaders are encouraged to become emotionally healthy.

     1   2   3   4   5   6   7   8   9   10

Our culture breeds spiritual and emotional health.

     1   2   3   4   5   6   7   8   9   10

I am walking in the Spirit and empowered by the Spirit.

1 2 3 4 5 6 7 8 9 10

I value my own emotional and relational health.

1 2 3 4 5 6 7 8 9 10

I am emotionally and relationally healthy.

1 2 3 4 5 6 7 8 9 10

In what ways are we striving and not thriving?

What needs to be addressed immediately?

How can we begin to equip our people for Spirit-empowered life and ministry?

How can we raise the value of leader health?

What needs to change in our culture?

How can I give greater value to my own spiritual and emotional health?

Next Steps

What can we do in the next 90 days to begin to implement necessary changes?

What will we do in the next six months?

What will we do in the next year?

SHIFT #5

FROM ACCUMULATING TO DEPLOYING

FROM ACCUMULATING TO DEPLOYING

Far too many lead the Church as if she were a business. We believe we are competing against other churches and ministries for people and resources. We aim to have greater market share than our competitors. We end up treating other Christian leaders in our community like competitors instead of comrades. With this mindset we engage in marketing and sales, with the idea that success equals accumulation. The more people, money, staff, and square-footage, the more successful we are. Then, when people leave our church or ministry to join another one, we demonize them for their disloyalty. We call them rebellious for not continuing to submit to our authority, and we disassociate with them for not helping to build our enterprise. Some leaders have gone as far as forcing staff to sign non-compete clauses when they leave, promising they won't start a new work within a certain square-mile radius of the church. And, in some cases, they are told that if they work for another church nearby, they are in sin.

What have we become? How did we begin to believe this was who we are?

The Church is not a business. The Church is a family. We are God's Family. Healthy families aim to raise and develop healthy children to become healthy young adults who are eventually able to leave their home and start a new family. This is what God intends for the Church as well. We are called to make disciples who can grow up into healthy spiritual leaders who are gladly sent out to join other works or start new works. The sign of a healthy church is not necessarily how big it gets, but how it raises up, equips, and sends people who are mature enough to "leave home" and start new spiritual families themselves.

The last shift we need to make is from accumulating people and resources to deploying sent ones to extend the Kingdom and fill all in all with the presence of Christ.

CHAPTER THIRTEEN

Changing the Scorecard

If we are going to make the shift from accumulating to deploying, we must change the scorecard. We do what we value. We value what we measure. And we celebrate what we believe matters most. We can talk and plan all we want about getting back to making disciples through these previous four shifts, but if we don't change our metrics, we will keep repeating the same mistakes.

Consider what you measure. Stop and think about the stories you love to tell, the heroes you make, and the things you celebrate. People are very observant. The people in your organization know what you most care about by what you most talk about, who you hold up as examples, and what your organization gets most excited about. I have learned that most people in churches are really good followers. Most are doing what they believe the leadership values.

A friend of mine who was visiting one of our Soma Family of Churches retreats remarked how different it felt compared to other retreats or conferences he had attended. He said that no one asked him about his church size or growth. They only asked about how he was doing emotionally and spiritually. He shared how refreshing that felt. That would not have always been the case for our family of churches, but in recent years we have spent more time on the health of leaders than almost everything else. It is something we care about and pay close attention to. It's on our scorecard. Now that you know some of my story, you know why this is the case. To be clear, our family of churches needs to also work hard on some other parts of the scorecard, but we are doing leader health far better than we did in the past. This example proves that people can discern what matters most by what you've made most important.

If another leader were visiting your organization, what would they say you value and measure?

Jesus' Scorecard

What did Jesus value? What did he measure? Who did he point to as an example? What was on Jesus' scorecard?[1]

Jesus made it clear that everything hangs on loving God and loving our neighbor as ourselves. Then, when asked who our neighbor is, Jesus told the story of the Good Samaritan to explain that we are called to generously love whoever is in our path. Jesus fully demonstrated this for us at the cross, where he showed God's love by dying for us. We can conclude that love of God, love of self (not selfishness), and love of others, including strangers and enemies, should shape the heart of our scorecard. But how do we define it more categorically?

First, Jesus called a few to follow him, and he invested significant time and energy in their lives for three years. Intentional disciple-making relationships must make the scorecard. Jesus also celebrated the widow who gave a mite, worth one-eighth of a penny, but it was all she had. Then, he gave himself up for us all. Generosity of spirit and possessions makes Jesus' scorecard. Jesus said he came to bring good news to the poor and the oppressed, and he even went as far as saying that whatever we do to the least of these, we do to him. It seems clear that caring for the poor, standing up for the oppressed, and being present with the lonely make the card. Jesus equipped his disciples for ministry and then commanded them to do the same with others. So equipping every follower of Jesus for ministry needs to be on our scorecard. Jesus shared how the Good Shepherd leaves the 99 sheep to go find the lost one. And then, before he ascended to heaven, he sent his followers to be his witnesses to Jerusalem, Judea, and the ends of the earth. So releasing and sending people on mission to make disciples of all nations is a key part of the scorecard as well.

Loving God, self, and others specifically through:

- Intentional disciple-making relationships
- Generosity of spirit and possessions
- Caring for the poor, the oppressed, and the lonely
- Equipping others for ministry
- Releasing and sending for mission

I'm sure we could come up with many more, but these are helpful categories as we think through what we value, measure, and celebrate.

Numbers aren't everything, but they do measure some things. We need other ways to discern how we're doing as well. So how do we shape our scorecard?

The organization that I lead, Saturate, takes leaders through a one-year Disciple-Making Lab.[2] We help churches and denominations develop disciple-making pathways, vehicles, tools, and environments, and we help them discern how to design culture that supports the development of disciple-making disciples. We use P.L.A.N. as an acrostic (Practices, Language, Artifacts, and Narratives).[3] An organization's P.L.A.N. shapes the culture and clarifies its scorecard.

Practices are the things we encourage people to engage in regular, normative ways. They might be spiritual practices, disciple-making practices, or unique practices your organization is aiming at. It's likely you already pay attention to and measure some of these practices, such as baptisms, giving, and involvement in key events or activities, but it might be helpful to reconsider how you measure some of these practices in light of the shifts we've discussed so far.

Language is not something we can measure with numbers, but it is something we can use to show what matters. Language needs to shape your scorecard because language creates culture or can erode the culture we're trying to create. If you say you believe the Church is the people of God, but use the phrase "go to church" or "It is so good to see you all at church today," are you not implying with your language that church is an event or a building instead of a people? If you believe worship is an all-of-life reality expression of our love for God, but only call the music set during your gatherings "worship," are you not implying that everything outside of singing is not worship? Do you believe in the priesthood of the saints and then use titles that communicate greater value for some over others?

Artifacts are visible reminders of what we value most. They can be captured in branding, signage, symbols, communication devices, and more. Israel was instructed by God to create markers like piles of stones (an ebenezer) to remember where God had miraculously provided. The instructions for how they were to design and build the temple were very specific so as to provide cues for how to remember and respond to God. Jesus specifically commanded his disciples to remember him through the bread and the wine. We need physical reminders to keep in front of us what matters most.

Narrative is all about the stories we tell, the heroes we make, and the history we remember. Stories inspire imagination and creativity. Stories capture memories. Jesus told stories to demonstrate his teaching and his values. It has been said that if you want to change a culture, give the people a new story.

We fully believed in the power of story at Doxa. In the early years, we shared a story almost every week because we wanted to change the overall narrative of what it meant to be the Church on mission in the everyday stuff of life. We had stories of success and failure to demonstrate that both are good because both demonstrate real people stepping out in faith, regardless of the outcome. We also recruited volunteer photographers to capture images (artifacts) and then post them on our social media channels to show and tell a story. Over time we even created a visual timeline of our church's story with key dates and descriptions marking key events in our history.

Let's apply a P.L.A.N. to the core values we've identified.[4]

Intentional Disciple-Making Relationships

Jesus spent considerable time with his disciples. As we've already clarified, he personally engaged in divine space with the Father; transparent space with Peter, James, and John; personal space with 12-20 men and women; social space at weddings, parties, and meals; and public space with the crowds. So how do you intentionally engage in a P.L.A.N. to build your scorecard around intentional relationship spaces?

At Doxa, we called every member to "Gather, Go, Give, and Grow" (Practice and Language). Through our disciple-making pathway we introduced them to what each of these meant and how they could engage them well. We also provided D.E.E.P.E.R. equipping around each step. After that, we asked every member to work through a personalized version of how they planned to live out this commitment in their disciple-making spaces. They filled out a form (Artifact) that asked some personal questions around these spaces to prepare them for an in-person interview. On the form and in the interview, we asked:

GATHER:

- How often do you plan to attend our larger gatherings on Sundays?
- How do you plan to engage in the liturgy for your own development as a disciple learning to make disciples?
- What do you think we could do to make the gathering more effective for your development?

GO:

- Are you in a missional community?
- How is your community helping you to be on mission to make new disciples?
- How can we better equip you, your missional community leaders, or your missional community to assist you in making disciples?

GIVE:

- How are you giving your time, talents, and treasures?
- Are you giving financially according to what the Scriptures instruct and how the Spirit is leading you?
- Do you know about your spiritual gifts, both who you are (people gifts) and what you can do (skill gifts)?
- Are you engaged in some expression of serving others with your gifts?

GROW:

- Are you in relationship with a few others who know your story and are regularly helping you grow through spiritual practices?
- How do you want to grow personally this year?
- And, what practices do you need better training in?

After the interview, we gave them a personalized development plan describing what they needed next (Artifact). Most people told us they had never been through a process that took their development so seriously. At least one Sunday a month, we tried to highlight one of the "Gs" through a story of life change (Narrative) as a result of someone stepping more fully into one of these disciple-making spaces and practices.

This process clearly communicated to our church family what being a part of Doxa entailed and what we truly valued, measured, and celebrated. It also helped us to keep recalibrating what we were doing to more effectively equip our people for each of the disciple-making spaces they were engaged in.

How are you designing a P.L.A.N. for intentional disciple-making relationships?

Generosity

Jesus spoke a lot about money. He wasn't shy about it. He knew that what we do with what we have reveals what we most love and care about. This is an area for many of us that lacks intentionality. Do you have a P.L.A.N. when it comes to developing disciples in generosity?

When I first stepped in to replant Doxa Church, our executive pastor, Tim, and I discussed how we might build metrics around giving that supported the disciple-making culture we wanted to create. Instead of just measuring how much money came in, we agreed that we wanted to measure how our disciple-making environment shaped people's growth in generosity. He came up with three categories (Language) for measuring our giving that would help us focus on growth in generosity: Stingy Steve, Average Joe, and Giver Gary. We wanted to see those who were not giving (Stingy Steves) grow in generosity and start giving. We wanted to see the average giver (Average Joe) grow in generosity by the percentage they gave each year. And we wanted the percentage of overall giving by a few large donors to decrease so the giving was carried by the many and not just a few (Giver Garys).

Whenever he and I sat down and looked at our finances, we asked, "Are Doxa members growing in generosity?" not "Is our overall giving increasing?" Over time we saw fewer Stingy Steves and more Average Joes. Our Average Joes grew in giving from 1.5% to 5% over three to four years. Giver Garys didn't decrease their giving, but they became a smaller percentage of our overall giving over the years. Our people did grow in generosity, and we could actually measure it.

In light of the past (Mars Hill), we also decided to be very transparent in regard to financial reports (our Narrative shaped this). So my salary was public knowledge, and we gave a financial update once a month (Artifact and Narrative). We also intentionally taught on giving at least twice a year so that we weren't just talking about it when we had financial needs. And, as I shared earlier, we shared a "Give" story on Sunday two to four times a year as well.

We also measured how much we as a church grew in giving money away to other churches and organizations. An accumulation mentality looks to spend more on yourselves and save more for the future of your own church. We agreed that if we wanted individuals to grow in generosity, the church needed to also grow in generosity. We grew from giving 5% away to giving almost 25% away over the years. I know of a wonderful church in Gainesville, Florida, who gives over 50% of their budget away to other ministries and mission works.

We not only gave money away. We also gave people away to serve other churches and to join new church plants.

How are you building a P.L.A.N. for a generosity scorecard?

Care for the Poor, the Oppressed, and the Lonely

Jesus called us to care for those who are often overlooked and cannot necessarily give us something in return. He told stories to make this Kingdom value very clear. One of the most compelling and convicting stories Jesus told was about those who will appear before him one day as he confronts them for not feeding him when he was hungry, clothing him when he was naked, and visiting him when he was in prison, saying that when we did not do it to one of the least of these, we did not do it to him. Jesus sees our care for the poor, the oppressed, and the lonely as an act of loving service to him.

With that said, how do we build and P.L.A.N. our scorecard around this?

I wonder what would happen if a church had to prove how it had reduced the tax burden in a city in order to maintain non-profit status. That is the reason we are given a status that frees us from the same taxes a for-profit company pays. We're supposed to be doing the kinds of things that taxes pay for. How is your church doing in this area? Have you become more committed to accumulating for your own sake than serving and giving for the sake of those in your community who are in need? Maybe lowering the tax burden should be part of our scorecard?

I remember hearing a story from a leader in Alabama. He, along with many others, had created new expressions of the Church through business. They helped people who didn't have the necessary history, capital, or expertise to start their own businesses. Many of these people would have remained in poverty had they not been given help. The investors also taught them how to lead their new businesses with Kingdom values so as to bring unique expressions of the Kingdom of God into that place. With every new business that started, a new Kingdom expression arose, and the city benefitted as well. When this leader realized he and his family were called to go to another place and do this again, the mayor reached out, concerned. He asked whether or not all the businesses were going to continue. This leader affirmed that none of it would be changing. The businesses would continue. The mayor was relieved as he shared that they would have had to raise taxes since the businesses contributed so much to the city's financial well-being.

The executive pastor who helped us devise a better way to measure giving, Tim, also had a huge heart for this. He, along with several others, built out what he called "Kingdom Causes" (Language) as a reminder of Jesus' heart for the poor, the oppressed, and the lonely. He made the case that any disciple of Jesus would be involved in serving the least of these. Tim began the charge to make sure we were leading our people to serve one or more Kingdom causes (Practices). He wanted to see us provide opportunities to care for foster children and the families who took them in. He also wanted us to care for those stuck in human trafficking. And finally, he wanted us to care for the homeless. In each instance, he built bridges to trustworthy organizations so that we could refer our people to serve in one or more of these places of need.

As I shared earlier, our greatest impact was with the foster care system. Every Christmas we invited everyone at Doxa to buy gift cards to give to foster children. Our people showed up! We gave so much that every local kid in foster care received

Christmas gifts. We even received a letter from the governor thanking us for our generosity (Artifact). We regularly shared the stories of lives changed as a result of our engagement and generosity (Narrative). Tim and a group of people who cared deeply for this cause set aside key events in our calendar to help our people become more aware of the needs in the foster care system in Washington. And, in partnership with many trustworthy organizations, the team came up with a way for every person in Doxa to be involved in this Kingdom Cause if they wanted to. I believe there are now at least 10 missional communities who provide care and support for foster families because of this initiative, and Doxa Church is now recognized in the region for their care for foster children and families.

What's your P.L.A.N. for building a scorecard around this important work?

Equipping Others for Ministry

If we are going to make the shift from accumulating people to deploying ministers, our scorecard must include equipping for ministry. This was front and center in Jesus' mind when he called his disciples to follow him. So how do we build a P.L.A.N. for this?

Language is a key part of it, but our practice must line up with our language. For example, I regularly say that every member is a minister and all of life is ministry. But I'll never forget when a business leader pulled me aside after a Sunday gathering. He said he loved our emphasis on calling everyone a minister and how we publicly commissioned people. However, he noted, "I have never observed us commissioning marketplace leaders, teachers, or civic leaders." He was calling out a deficiency in our scorecard. Our language was good; we called all people ministers. But it didn't line up with our practice; we were only commissioning some people to some kinds of ministry. Publicly commissioning people for the ministry they are called to in everyday life is a powerful way to affirm that you believe everyone is a minister.

But language is not enough. We must have the practice of actually equipping people as part of our scorecard. At Doxa, we asked ourselves how we'd measure this. We could measure how often we provided equipping events and how many people participated. We also could make sure that we provided D.E.E.P.E.R. equipping for everything we expected people to do. We communicated in our "meet and greet" lunch (for people visiting Doxa) that our mission was to equip everyone to be a disciple of Jesus who makes disciples. We then let them know they could start their equipping journey the very next week by beginning our disciple-making pathway. I remember when we first started providing monthly equipping opportunities for our members. A lot of people attended, but the majority were men! Some of you would be very happy since you don't see many men coming out for training. However, my concern was that we were missing the women. I asked where all the women were, and one of the men said, "They're home with the kids." With some anger in my heart, I told him and the other fathers that next time they needed to stay home with the kids so their wives could attend. We came up with a better solution than that by providing childcare so that both men and women would be able to attend and be equipped.

Language and practices, but what would be the artifacts and narratives? People actually doing the work of ministry and experiencing the outcomes.

One of the churches in the Soma Family decided to start measuring the practice of having Jesus conversations. They had trained their people how to get into and have Jesus conversations, but the proof would not be in how many attended the training but in the actual conversations they had. They recognized, as is important to do when creating a scorecard, that there are some things we can control and other things we can't. We can control whether we talk about Jesus or not. We can't control whether people come to faith or not. When I am coaching a leader, I often encourage them to distinguish between a work goal and a faith goal. A work goal is something we can do. A faith goal is what we pray for and look to God to do. This church asked members to pray for opportunities to have Jesus conversations with people. Whenever they had one of those conversations, they informed the church leadership. The church set a goal of having 1,000 Jesus conversations in one year. They had a visual display in their gathering space that kept track. That year they had 1,020 unique Jesus conversations. That year also set a new standard for the number of people coming to faith.

Baptism is also important to have on our scorecard, but if equipping people for ministry is a value, we might want to rethink how we measure baptism. What if we measured how many people were baptized by the person who led them to Christ? What if we also measured how many groups participated in someone's journey to faith? At Doxa Church we made the shift from elders baptizing new believers to our members baptizing those they've led to Christ. We also invited the community of people who were a part of a person coming to faith to come forward and gather around the person being baptized. In doing so, we demonstrated that we were equipping disciples to make disciples (which includes baptizing as Jesus clearly stated), as well as training missional communities to work together to make disciples in community (valuing the personal and social spaces for disciple-making). This creates a strong visual scorecard. We also informed people that their baptism was their commission to go and make disciples as well. I remember the first time at Doxa when someone said, "I was baptized by my friend last year. Now I want to introduce you to my friend who I have the privilege of baptizing today." We were seeing second-generation disciple-making and publicly showing the value of equipping for that.

Releasing and Sending for Mission

As I've said before, healthy families raise up healthy children who become healthy adults who can leave home to start healthy families. The same is true for churches committed to disciple-making and deploying. If we never see people leave to start new works, we have failed at our work. Of course, not everyone should leave, as some need to stay to continue raising up and sending out. However, we do need to flip the scorecard here. Are we content to see more people stay than leave to start new works? Imagine you're a parent whose kids never leave because they never want to grow up and take responsibility? Is that what we've done in the Church as well?

The success of Jesus' disciple-making was observed in the disciples not staying in the upper room but being anointed and sent by the Holy Spirit to be his witnesses. When the persecution happened in Jerusalem, we read that everyone except the apostles were scattered, and they all preached the gospel everywhere they went.

What about us? What kind of culture are we building? What kind of scorecard are we creating? Are we trying to grow a big church that keeps everyone? Or, are we aiming at a church that wants to send as many out on mission as possible? I have far too many conversations with church leaders who are reluctant to send. I also have too many conversations with people who wish their leaders would bless and release them. Again, I come back to what I shared in the introduction: COVID-19 revealed how poorly we have prepared our people to take responsibility for being the Church wherever God has placed them. Changing the scorecard in this area starts with reframing the mission of Jesus as the responsibility of everyone in the church.

When we first started Doxa, we went through a series from 1 Peter entitled, *Church Everywhere*. We needed to reframe who the Church is and how we are sent on mission every day, everywhere. We had a very talented artist create a large map of our region that was cut into several segments. When we started the series, we placed each segment on an easel outside our gathering center. After teaching about how each one of us is a living stone making up a spiritual house that is scattered throughout the region (Language), we had everyone sign their name in the segment of our region where they wanted to bring the presence of Jesus. Some signed it where they live, some where they learn or work, and some both. All the pieces of the map were reassembled and hung as a backdrop on the stage while we continued the series (Artifact). Each week we would bring a piece of the map down, place it on an easel on the stage, and invite people from that region to share how they hoped Jesus would work through them in that space. Then we prayed and commissioned them to be on mission there (Practice).

Before we put a map piece back up, our artist painted the map segment with a portion of the face of Christ. Eventually, the full picture was revealed, and it showed the full face of Jesus over the entire map of our region, demonstrating our desire to see Jesus fill all in all (Language). That map still hangs in the entrance area of the space where Doxa gathers as a reminder of the origin story (Narrative) and the ongoing vision to deploy everyone on mission every day. That learning process seeded movement and missional thinking in our people.

I often wondered, "What if we committed ourselves to regularly commissioning people as a normal practice?" For instance, what if every fall, we commissioned and sent teachers and students to be missionaries at school and college? What if every November we commissioned people working in politics or some other form of public service? What if every January, we commissioned the marketplace leaders? I'm sure you could come up with more strategic moments to commission different people. Let's consider how we could make that a regular practice.

Also think about the language you need to create or emphasize to change your sending scorecard. For example, "We believe we're growing as a church if we're losing people through sending;" "We don't want to fill buildings; we want to fill our city with the presence of Christ;" "Our job is to equip and mobilize people from Sunday to Everyday;" "Every member is a missionary." Craig Tuck, who gives leadership to Mission Charleston, an effort to unify the Church in Charleston toward gospel saturation, likes to say, "Sunday is the harmony that supports the melody of God's people on mission every day, Monday through Saturday."[5]

The goal for this is that people begin to see that it is normal for people to be released and sent. I remember one of the things we often said at Soma in the early days was: "We're all getting ready to be sent. The question isn't whether we will be sent. The question is when are we leaving, and where are we going?"

What will it take for this to be your scorecard? What P.L.A.N. needs to be put in place to make this your new norm?

We need to make the shift from accumulating to deploying, and that shift starts in you!

NOTES

1. This is a good exercise for a leadership team to go through. Ask this question with your team and see what they come up with. Then consider your culture and how closely it resembles Jesus' scorecard.

2. If you are interested in a Saturate Disciple-Making Lab, go to saturatetheworld.com for more information.

3. Catapult came up with the P.L.A.N. acronym. Catapult is an innovation agency, with a full-service shop, that helps leaders scale and activate their vision. You can learn more about them at https://wearecatapult.org/.

4. We could identify more categories and many more ways to measure, but due to the limit of space, we will just provide some examples for these core values.

5. For more information about Mission Charleston, go to: https://missionchs.org/. And to hear from Craig, check out the video about Mission Charleston at https://saturatetheworld.com/hubs/.

CHAPTER FOURTEEN

Surrender—This Starts with You

Every great move of God seems to begin with repentance and surrender.

Whenever I meet with leaders who want to bring change and transition to their context, I remind them that, in most cases, people faithfully followed them to where they are now. Your church or ministry, if you've been leading it for a while, is where it is because people followed your leadership and your example. So any change that is going to happen must first begin with you. You need repentance, and you need to surrender.

Unfortunately, we have given the word *repent* a bad rap. The word *repent* in the Greek is *metanoia*, which means having a change of mind. I hope as you have been reading, some things in your mind have changed. Maybe you have a different view of God. Maybe your thoughts about what a disciple is has shifted. Hopefully, your perspective about yourself and the work God has for you in the future has changed. I hope you see more clearly than ever before.

Repentance is a gift. It's not about groveling in guilt and shame. Repentance is about God giving you new thoughts, new dreams, new visions that help you see that God is doing a new thing in you and wants to do a new thing *through* you. Without repentance there is no change. We don't do a 180 return to disciple-making without personally doing a 180 return to God and his ways for building his Church.

Before God will do something through you, he first does something to you. He wants to give you the gift of repentance and then call you to surrender your life to him afresh.

Surrender Personally

Let's start with you and God. Are you lovingly attaching to God in life-giving ways? Are you making space for God to meet with you and remind you of how deeply loved you are by him? Do you need to repent from wrong thoughts or beliefs about God? Do you have any other gods before God in your life that you are entrusting yourself to or looking to for your ultimate hope? Are there any practices that you need to re-engage in afresh? Do you need to block out a regular time for silence and solitude?

Years ago, I recognized that these were not regular practices in my life as a leader. To kick-start my heart in these practices, I set aside one night and day every month for six months where I would go away the night before and then wake up to spend the entire day in silence and solitude. Eventually, I began to integrate shorter but regular segments of silence and solitude into my weekly rhythms and then engage in one to two days of silence and solitude a quarter. I also began the regular practice of fasting and prayer one day a week with longer times (several days) when needed. The practices of abstinence (silence, solitude, fasting, sabbath) can also help us confront areas of unhealthy consumption in our lives.

Do you need to address any areas where you are over-consuming or consuming things that are destructive? Are you walking in the fullness and power of the Holy Spirit? Do you know the Father's love for you experientially? Are you submitting to the power of the Spirit to overcome sin and temptation throughout your day? Are you experiencing the anointing of the Spirit to proclaim the good news of Jesus? Do you believe and walk in the power of the Spirit to pray for others' healing or deliverance?

How about your emotional and relational health? Are you attending to your heart? Do you have trusted friends or counselors you can truly show up with and not feel the need to hide or perform? Are you aware of your feelings, needs, and desires, and are you going to God and others in healthy ways to get what you need and want? Or have you been going to unhealthy places or sources instead?

This starts with you. Locate yourself and pay attention to the story you are believing. Consider what you've been doing to address your needs. Repent. Turn to God and surrender to him. Get help where you need it. You can't lead people to a place you have not been or are not presently in.

Surrender to Make Disciples

Next, are you leading by example? Are you engaging in the relational spaces to grow in attachment to God and others? Are you spending time with the people you're developing as well as with people who don't yet follow Jesus? Are you actively sharing your faith? Are you making disciples who make disciples?

Most leaders who report that disciple-making is a weakness in their church or ministry also admit being weak at it personally—because most were never discipled to make disciples themselves. Bible schools and seminaries don't usually equip people to be disciple-makers. They equip us to be good theologians, teachers, and caregivers. And the method used in most schools is nothing close to D.E.E.P.E.R.. So be kind to yourself. There is a reason you may not yet be effective at this. However, the invitation of Jesus stands before you ... Will you follow him in the ways he's leading you to shift how you make disciples?

Start by admitting your struggle. Invite the Holy Spirit to be your teacher and guide. Surrender to the Spirit, and invite him to lead you to others who are equipped and effective at making disciples. Then ask them for help.[1] Don't stay alone, and don't try to do it alone.

Several years ago, we created one-year disciple-making learning communities for church leaders in the Seattle area. We called the initiative Saturate the Sound. We had over 100 leaders participate in 10 different cohorts (one for each region we were working in). We started by making sure we had created a safe place where leaders could be honest about their personal struggles and their church challenges. We made it safe to tell the truth about what they didn't know or couldn't do. We first helped them learn some basic disciple-making practices to personally implement. We wanted them to be able to lead their churches by example, not just through explaining. As they led by example, we also helped them to bring change to their church through equipping their people to become disciple-making disciples. One pastor admitted to his church that he had never personally shared his story with an unbeliever. He went on to share it in front of the whole church, and he let them know they were going to train everyone to share their story with Jesus as the hero. Each week they had another person come up front to share their story. Eventually, he and many others in his church had the opportunity to share their stories with unbelievers. He reported that they saw many come to faith in Jesus as a result.[2]

Like these pastors, you won't lead people to do what you are not doing yourself. First, you won't have the ability to, and second, you won't have the integrity to. Start by surrendering to the Spirit to be a disciple-maker.

Then you will be able to surrender to the Spirit what you are leading as well.

Surrender the Ministry

I hope that after having read this, you will have some clarity about the things that need to change in the church or ministry you lead. Start with a prayer of surrender to the Holy Spirit. Surrender the ministry you lead to the Spirit's leadership, empowerment, and direction. Invite the Spirit to show you what needs to change, how the Spirit wants you to change it, and when you are to bring about change.

Commit yourself with those around you to fully surrender to the Spirit to lead a ministry that leads people to truly attach to God and others in disciple-making spaces through the spiritual practices. Commit to holistically equip people in the diverse expression of who Jesus is, for ministry in all of life. Invite the Spirit to teach you how to lead others in spirit-empowered ministry. Confront any culture of emotional or relational unhealth, and go get help if needed (like I wish I had when I started Doxa Church). Change your scorecard to represent the heart and call of Jesus.

Do this with those you lead, but start with your own posture of surrender before you call others to join you. You may even want to publicly do this as a church. People are often resistant to change. However, humble leaders who can admit they've been wrong will create an environment of grace and courage in which others can step forward in new ways. When God's people repent and surrender together, they put themselves in a posture for God to do remarkable things through them.

Surrender Your Future

Some of you are being prepared to be sent. God has been getting you ready with a fresh vision for a new work. For some of you, that is a new ministry, a new non-profit, or a new business venture for the Kingdom. Others of you are being prepared to sow the seeds of the gospel in a new place so that a new expression of the Church will spring up there. This book is one of the many things that God has put in your life to stir you up for what he wants to do through you.

Surrender your future to Jesus. Invite the Spirit to lead you to take next steps. Get plenty of counsel, assessment, training, and coaching. Don't do it alone. Reach out to others who have gone before you, and learn from them. Ask God to give you partners, so you do it together in community on mission. Connect to a reputable organization with a track record of the things I've written about, especially the fourth shift from striving to thriving.

I pray you will find strength in surrender. May the Spirit anoint, fill, and empower you to be a disciple who makes disciples and a leader who leads disciple-making movements.

I pray as you take new steps forward that you will stay in a posture of surrender to the Father's love, Jesus' leadership, and the power and guidance of the Holy Spirit as you return to disciple-making in your own life and ministry.

NOTES

1. Saturate provides coaching, training, and intensive learning environments if you would like additional help in making disciples. Go to *https:// saturatetheworld.com* and consider one of our offerings that might serve you.

2. If you would like to start similar learning communities or look to join one, please reach out to us at Saturate. We are willing to share the entire curriculum we created for Saturate the Sound.

CHAPTER FIFTEEN

Planning Your Way Forward

Use this section to capture all your work so it is in one place.

DISCIPLE-MAKING PLAN

Definition of a Disciple:

Disciple-Making Pathway:

EQUIPPING STRATEGY

Which skills do we want to equip disciples with?

How will we include the five gifts as we demonstrate and equip?

How will we build out D.E.E.P.E.R. forms of equipping?

PLAN FOR ATTACHING IN RELATIONAL SPACES

Which relational spaces do we plan to intentionally engage in or build for the sake of helping people attach to God and others in our context?

Which practices will help us lead and equip our people to engage in each of those spaces?

CHANGING YOUR CONTEXT FROM STRIVING TO THRIVING

How will we create and lead a culture that makes it natural and normal to walk in the Spirit and engage in Spirit-empowered ministry?

How will we pursue our own emotional and relational health, and how will we create a culture where it is normative to pursue emotional health as leaders?

CHANGING THE SCORECARD

Considering all this, what do we want to be on the scorecard?

How will we P.L.A.N. to make this happen?

What will be our PRACTICES?

How will we use LANGUAGE to reinforce what we measure?

What ARTIFACTS will we use or create?

How will we engage NARRATIVE to build the scorecard?

About the Author

As the Executive Director of Saturate and founding leader of the Soma Family of Churches, Jeff Vanderstelt gets to spend his days doing what he loves – mentoring leaders and equipping the Church in the gospel and missional living. Additionally, Jeff is on the leadership team of Saturate the Sound, a local church collective focused on gospel saturation in the Puget Sound. Jeff has authored *Saturate*, *Gospel Fluency*, and *Making Space*.

He and Jayne, his wife, have three children: Haylee, Caleb, and Maggie. Connect with Jeff on X and Instagram @JeffVanderstelt

List of Resources

Gospel Fluency: Speaking the Truths of Jesus into the Everyday Stuff of Life by Jeff Vanderstelt

Gospel Fluency Handbook and Video Series by Jeff Vanderstelt and Ben Connelly

Saturate: Being Disciples of Jesus in the Everyday Stuff of Life by Jeff Vanderstelt

Saturate Field Guide and Video Series by Jeff Vanderstelt and Ben Connelly

Disciple-Making Pathway Video Series by Jeff Vanderstelt

Making Space: Exploring Proverbs for What Matters Most Study and Videos by Jeff Vanderstelt

Gospel Through the Heart: Feeling Your Way to Jesus by Jeff Vanderstelt and Jeff Schulte (Coming in 2024)

Many of these resources and hundreds more are available through Saturate membership. Go to saturatetheworld.com/180-disciple-making to learn more.

Revive.

Refresh.

- ⌐ ACCELERATE YOUR IMPACT
- ⌐ WORLD'S LARGEST LIBRARY OF MULTIPLICATION CONTENT
- ⌐ COMMUNITY WITH A COMMON CAUSE
- ⌐ WORLD CLASS GATHERINGS OF MULTIPLIERS

☰XPONENTIAL⌐

Register now at
exponential.org

Made in United States
Orlando, FL
16 June 2024